POLICE SYSTEMS OF EUROPE

POLICE SYSTEMS OF EUROPE

A SURVEY OF SELECTED POLICE ORGANIZATIONS

By

HAROLD K. BECKER, D. CRIM.

Professor of Criminology
Director, Center for Criminal Justice
Department of Criminology
California State University
Long Beach, California

CHARLES C THOMAS • PUBLISHER
Springfield • Illinois • USA

Published and Distributed Throughout the World by
CHARLES C THOMAS • PUBLISHER
BANNERSTONE HOUSE
301-327 East Lawrence Avenue, Springfield, Illinois, U.S.A.

© *1973, by* CHARLES C THOMAS • PUBLISHER
ISBN 0-398-02734-X
Library of Congress Catalog Card Number: 72-92162

With THOMAS BOOKS *careful attention is given to all details of
manufacturing and design. It is the Publisher's desire to present books
that are satisfactory as to their physical qualities and artistic possibilities
and appropriate for their particular use.* THOMAS BOOKS *will be true
to those laws of quality that assure a good name and good will.*

Printed in the United States of America
EE-11

To Donna, Ann, Harold, and Alice
    for their courage, stamina, and perseverance

OTHER BOOKS BY HAROLD K. BECKER

Issues in Police Administration 1970
Law Enforcement: A Selected Bibliography 1968 (Co-Authored)
New Dimensions in Criminal Justice 1968 (Co-Authored)

For many are called, but few are chosen.

— New Testament
The Gospel According to
Saint Matthew 22:14

... you must not forsake the ship in a tempest, because you cannot rule and keep down the winds . . . and that which you cannot turn to good, you can at least make less bad.

— Book I of *Utopia* by
Sir Thomas More (1516)

PREFACE

WITH THE PUBLICATION OF RESEARCH DATA by the President's Commission on Law Enforcement and Administration of Justice in 1967 and subsequent commission criticism[1] of police practices and behavior, renewed vigor has been established toward police research. Federal funds were initially made available through the Law Enforcement Assistance Act of 1965 and have continued to the present time, modified in the form of Title I, Part C, Omnibus Crime Control and Safe Streets Act of 1968.

Academic institutions, as well as private industry, have become involved in varying types of police studies. Inquiry into criminal justice is concerning itself, in part, with questions of what "is" in fact the position of police today[2] and what "ought to be" the development of police in the future. This complexity of police inquiry is analogous to the position of public administration in the stormy debates between the "is" characteristics of reality and the "ought to be" characteristics of what reality should be.[3] A sum-

1. As an example see *Rights in Conflict*, a Report Submitted by Daniel Walker, Director of the Chicago Study Team, to the National Commission on the Causes and Prevention of Violence (New York: Bantam Books, 1968). For historical interest see the National Commission on Law Observance and Enforcement (George W. Wickersham, Chairman), Report No. 11: *Lawlessness in Law Enforcement* and Report No. 14: *Police* (Washington: Government Printing Office, 1931); and a review of the *Police Report* by August Vollmer, "Abstract of the Wickersham Police Report," *Journal of Criminal Law and Criminology*, vol. 22, January, 1932.

2. See for example, James Q. Wilson: *Varieties of Police Behavior: The Management of Law and Order in Eight Communities* (Cambridge: Harvard University Press, 1968); less critical, James Cramer: *The World's Police* (London: Cassell and Company, Ltd., 1964); and the President's Commission on Law Enforcement and the Administration of Justice: *Task Force Report: The Police* (Washington: Government Printing Office, 1967).

3. See Dwight Waldo: *The Study of Public Administration* (New York: Random House, 1963), pp. 43-45 for a review of logical positivism; Herbert A. Simon: *Administrative Behavior* (New York: Macmillan Co., 1947); and Simon et al.: *Public Administration* (New York: Alfred A. Knopf, Inc., 1950), ch. I.

mation of the argument would develop two models in which a policeman could be conceptualized: (1) as law enforcer, and (2) as social agent.

Therefore, it is the general responsibility of police research, as in other areas of inquiry, to establish a broad data base from which conceptualization of formal police organization has a closer fit with societal needs.

Woodrow Wilson conceptualized the utility of comparative analysis in the following statement, "If I see a murderous fellow sharpening a knife cleverly, I can borrow his way of sharpening the knife without borrowing his probable intention to commit murder with it. . . ."[4] Wilson's statement describes the methodology of the comparative approach in its three fundamental parts: (1) the use of information, (2) the recording of observations, and finally (3) participation in the activity.[5]

The modern comparative approach is an adaptation from cultural anthropology and is applied to the study of social problems by other disciplines.

It is necessary to appreciate the relation of man and his culture before one applies Woodrow Wilson's concept of "borrowing methods without borrowing intentions." The utility of comparative analysis, when applied to the study of police behavior, individual and organizational, cannot be separated from its cultural context. Man cannot be studied apart from the culture that surrounds him. Man "and his extensions" are "one interrelated system."[6] So it is in the study of police organization as it affects the average citizen.

During this author's study in Europe and England one observation was repeatedly made, "Some problems are similar from police organization to police organization regardless of culture." The following are examples: working conditions, pay, types of crime, deployment of personnel, and employee job satisfaction. Techniques to resolve these problems do, however, differ.

---

4. Woodrow Wilson: "The Study of Administration," *Political Science Quarterly,* ch. 2, pp. 197–222, June 1887.

5. D. F. Pocock: *Social Anthropology* (London: Sheed and Ward, 1961).

6. Edward T. Hall: *The Hidden Dimensions* (New York: Anchor Books, 1969), p. 188.

It is within the phenomena of different techniques in resolving similar problems that the value of comparative police systems can be found. In writing about one such institution, Seymour Lipset has stressed that

> ... it is necessary to know how it differs from the comparable institution in other cultures. Only when one knows what is unique on a comparative scale can one begin to ask significant questions about causal relationships within a country. Hence, even that most particularistic of all social scientists, the historian, can learn much about American history by studying the history of somewhat comparable foreign nations at equivalent points in their development. And if this is true for the historian, then it is even more valid for the rest of us.[7]

---

7. Seymour Martin Lipset: *The First Nation* (New York: Basic Books, Inc., 1963), p. 348.

ACKNOWLEDGMENTS

THIS WRITER WISHES TO EXPRESS his appreciation to Mr. Philip John Stead, Bramshill Police College, England, who so graciously made available college facilities and suggestions. For their assistance in many ways I am especially indebted to Mr. Dennis Brett of Bramshill Library, Police College, England; Mr. John Minnick, Legal Attaché, American Embassy, London, England; Superintendent Burrows, Liverpool and Bootle Training Center, Liverpool, England; Superintendent J. P. de B. Kennard, Warwickshire Constabulary, Warwickshire, England; Mr. Henri Feraud, Interpol Library, Saint-Cloud, France; the Danish Ministry of Justice, Copenhagen, Denmark; Sergeant Borge Jennssen, Public Information Division, Copenhagen, Denmark; Dr. Franz Chrudimak, police administrator, Vienna, Austria; Mr. Einar Hjellemo, police administrator, Oslo, Norway; Chief Inspector Jelte Kuipers, Amsterdam police, Netherlands; Mr. Beek, interpreter and assistant to the Legal Attaché, American Embassy, Brussels, Belgium; to the police in Stockholm, Sweden, and Zürich, Switzerland; and to the generosity of the California State University, particularly the Department of Criminology—all of whom helped make this research possible.

Many thanks to the Police Institute at Hiltrup, Germany for the use of library facilities, and to all the American Consulate personnel and police personnel in Europe who contributed to this research; and especially to my wife, Donna, and our three children, who lived like gypsies for ten months in Europe and England.

The views presented in this research are, of course, my own and are not the responsibility of any of the kind people who assisted me along the way.

Long Beach, California   HAROLD K. BECKER

CONTENTS

APPENDICES

POLICE SYSTEMS OF EUROPE

PART 1

THE SIGNIFICANCE AND AIMS OF COMPARATIVE POLICE SYSTEMS

CHAPTER 1

OBJECTIVES

THE FOLLOWING OBJECTIVE is to be pursued in this survey:
To contribute to the comparative study of police administration through the analysis of formal police organization.
The formal organization is studied with reference to political traits and legal characteristics. Selected cultural phenomena will be reflected in the political–legal description and act as the environment in which the formal organization functions.

A conceptual model was constructed in this study to ascertain the homological characteristics dealing with similarities and differences of police systems. Selected phenomena were developed to describe the interface of homological characteristics and a culture scheme [1] reference to view the following categories:

1. Organizational goals
2. Means to reach goals, i.e., procedures, personnel, etc.
3. Costs, i.e., monies directed to police force and how spent
4. Model, on a scale from military to civilian
5. Administrative process, i.e. centralization as opposed to civilian control or influence [2]

Thus, ". . . for those who seek to understand and improve their own systems, it is always useful to consider other systems in relation to their own.[3]

1. As an empirical tool see Gabriel Almond: "Comparative Systems," *Journal of Politics, 18*:391–409, 1959.
2. Based on Edward S. Quade, "Progress and Problems in Systems Analysis," in Robert T. Golembiewski and Frank Gibson: *Managerial Behavior and Organizational Demands: Management as a Linking of Levels of Interaction* (Chicago: Rand McNally and Co., 1967), pp. 401–430.
3. Marshall I. Goldman: *Comparative Economic System* (New York: Random House, 1964), p. 458.

Comparative Method

The comparative method, sometimes referred to by sociologists as the *ex post facto* design,[4] is used in this study to investigate social phenomena when ". . . one cannot always select and control the factors necessary to study cause and effect relations in an artificial laboratory situation."[5] The comparative method is a development of identifying differences and similarities as expressed by John Stuart Mill in the 1800's, in that, "If two or more instances of the phenomenon under investigation have only one circumstance in common, the circumstance in which alone all the instances agree, is the cause (or effect) of the given phenomenon."[6]

Participant Observation

The technique of observation has ". . . been contributed mainly by social anthropology, where it has frequently taken the form of *participant observation*. In this form of observation the observer takes on, to some extent at least, the role of a member of the group and participates in its functioning."[7]

Organizational permission was given to this researcher to participate in various types of police activities, such as walking the "beat" with the area policeman, patrolling in police vehicles, and becoming involved in police programs. Participant observation was thus directed at the patrolman level of police work. Observation and interaction took place in all types of work situations as well as informal social gatherings.

Information was recorded which described the following factors: (1) characteristics of the participants, (2) the setting, and (3) the social behavior.[8]

---

4. William J. Goode and Paul K. Hatt: *Methods in Social Research* (New York: McGraw-Hill Book Co., 1952), p. 86.

5. Deobold B. Van Dalen: *Understanding Educational Research* (New York: McGraw-Hill Book Co., 1962), p. 200.

6. John Stuart Mill: *A System of Logic* (New York: Harper & Bros., 1846), p. 224.

7. Claire Selltiz et al.: *Research Methods in Social Relations* (New York: Holt, Rinehart and Winston, 1961), p. 207.

8. *Ibid.*, pp. 209–210.

Police Organization

It has been stated that "we are born in organizations, educated by organizations, and most of us spend much of our lives working for organizations." [9] All industrial societies, in which large urbanization has taken place, maintain formal organizations for the enforcement of rules, regulations, and public safety. "Some modern nations have been police states; all, however, are policed societies." [10] Regardless of political, cultural, and nationalistic characteristics there appears a continuity in industrial societies, and that is: *organized police systems.*

Organizations are complex structures consisting of many elements. It has been suggested that we think ". . . about organization . . . as a universe with its full complement of solar systems, galaxies, and individual planets. Such an analogy may be helpful because it emphasizes that any large scale entity must be composed of a series of subsystems." [11]

These subsystems would include, but would not be limited to, the following: a sociometric network of private likes and dislikes toward others; a functional network dependent on special skills and knowledge; then a grid of centers where decisions are really made, where may be found a pattern of power, and channels of communication can be observed.[12]

The complexity of organization is further established when one considers the influence exerted by the organization on the individual worker and, in return, the influence of the individual on the organization. No conclusive evidence has been developed that determines the influence of organizations on people. Stated more explicitly: "Do organizations change people?" [13]

---

9. Amitai Etzioni: *Modern Organizations* (Englewood Cliffs, N.J.: Prentice-Hall, Inc., 1964), p. 1.
10. Allan Silver, "The Demand for Order in Civil Society: A Review of Some Themes in the History of Urban Crime, Police, and Riots," in David J. Bordua (ed.): *Police: Six Sociological Essays* (New York: John Wiley and Sons, Inc., 1967), p. 6.
11. John M. Pfiffner and Frank P. Sherwood: *Administrative Organization* (Englewood Cliffs, N. J.: Prentice-Hall, Inc., 1960), p. 33.
12. *Ibid.*, p. 16.
13. Ivar Berg, "Do Organizations Change People?" in Leonard Sayles: *Individualism and Big Business* (New York: McGraw-Hill Book Co., Inc., 1963), pp. 61–65.

In viewing autocratic organizations Gilbert and Levinson ascertained that personalities of the personnel fitted in with the character of the organization [14] and that ". . . behavior was similarly consonant with the organization, the beliefs and the personalities of the people." [15]

Blau has indicated that an ". . . organization does not remain fixed according to the formal blueprint, but always evolves into new forms. Conditions change, problems arise, and in the course of coping with them, the members of the organization establish new procedures . . . , thereby modifying the structure." [16]

Considering the complexity of police organization, which is in line with the general complexity of all organizations, there arises a myriad of choices by which to view a police structure.

Comparative Culture Analysis

The study of police organization on a comparative basis within one culture has been well established in the disciplines of sociology, political science, and public administration. The literature is well documented with intra–cultural studies. Intra–cultural research, however, is by definition limited to general cultural patterns of the society being investigated. Organizational structure, goals, policies, and procedures generally fit within the cultural restraints. Comparison of similar organizations within a general cultural universe does not reveal differences and similarities as being *that* uniquely characteristic of the organization being researched.

Inter–cultural studies, however, emphasize the differences *and* similarities. The social scientists seek to develop, empirically, theories that interrelate functions, structures, and behavior with one another and with the experiment as a whole. Collecting in-

14. D. Gilbert and D. J. Levinson, "Role Performance, Ideology and Personality in Mental Hospital Aides," in M. Greenblat, D. J. Levinson, and R. Williams (eds.): *The Patient and the Mental Hospital* (New York: The Free Press of Glencoe, 1957), pp. 197–208. Also see Ivar Berg: "Role Personality and Social Structure: The Nurse in the General Hospital," Ph.D. dissertation, Harvard University (Cambridge, Mass.), 1960.
15. Berg, *op. cit.*, p. 61.
16. Peter M. Blau: *Bureaucracy in Modern Society* (New York: Random House, 1956), p. 57.

formation from ". . . several systems also helps to reduce the possibility that the same intervening variable will continue to be present to mislead the researcher. Thus accumulating a number of studies on the same topic in various countries helps to substantiate . . . theories by demonstrating that they are valid cross–nationally." [17]

Hall, already referred to (see Preface), has poignantly illustrated the interaction of culture, man, and organization in this passage:

> . . . no matter how hard man tries it is impossible for him to divest himself of his own culture, for it has penetrated to the roots of his nervous system and determines how he perceives the world. Most of culture lies hidden and is outside voluntary control, making up the warp and weft of human existence.
>
> Man and his extensions constitute one interrelated system. It is a mistake of the greatest magnitude to act as though man were one thing, and his house or his cities, his technology or his language were something else.[18]

---

17. Jorgen Rasmussen: *The Process of Politics* (New York: Atherton Press, Inc., 1969), pp. 5–6.

18. Edward T. Hall: *The Hidden Dimension* (New York: Doubleday and Co., 1969), p. 188.

CHAPTER 2

ASSUMPTIONS AND LIMITATIONS

THE PRINCIPAL AIM OF THIS RESEARCH is to view the formal organization of the police. Inquiry shall be directed toward such characteristics as structure, processes, and objectives.[19]

ORGANIZATION

The formal organization of the various police systems will be considered as a planned grouping of people and things—the result of conscious decision making. For the purpose of this study, formal organization will also include ". . . behavior of individuals and groups influenced by . . . organization prescriptions."[20]

An inter–cultural approach will be used in that culturally distinct communities have been selected for our survey. Conscious preconceptions on the part of the researcher are anticipated to be kept to a minimum by systemically identifying the what, where, and how characteristics that describe formal organization.

This study acknowledges the complexity of organization and the constant change of organizational structure, personnel, and values. We might liken our subject to a patient undergoing examination. Here it is the desire of the researcher to state the external physical description of the "patient" in lieu of conducting major surgery to view him internally.[21] The following assumptions are to be pursued in this study:

1. ORGANIZATION WILL BE STUDIED IN TERMS OF STRUCTURE, PROCESSES, AND OBJECTIVES.

---

19. Joseph A. Litterer: *The Analysis of Organizations* (New York: John Wiley & Sons, Inc., 1965), p. 135.
20. *Ibid.*, p. 136.
21. Nigel Walker: *A Short History of Psychotherapy in Theory and Practice* (New York: Noonday Press, 1959), pp. 4–5.

2. POLICE BEHAVIOR WILL BE DESCRIBED WHERE APPROPRIATE.

CULTURE

The concept of culture in this study is to be used as a technique of analysis. It is not the purpose of this research to enter into the dialogue of A. L. Kroeber and Clyde Kluckhohn who analyzed 164 definitions of culture,[22] but to assume the general idea of culture to be "the abstracted non–biological conditions of human life—'artifacts, mentifacts.' " [23]

It has been stated that man's behavior "in all aspects important to understanding him as a human being, is always related to and somehow a reflection of the characteristics of the social–cultural world in which it happens to function." [24] This position is sometimes called cultural determination,[25] or—for the purposes of this survey—cultural expectations.

THE RELATION OF CULTURE TO ORGANIZATION

Two applications of culture to the study of organization have been cited by Pfiffner and Sherwood in the following:

> First, it is important to recognize that no organization can be isolated from its cultural environment. That is, organization as social organisms must operate within the framework of the larger cultural system. As a consequence, the alternatives in any given situation are greatly limited by their congruity with the values of the total culture.
>
> A second application of the culture concept is to consider the organization as a subculture. In such an instance, the culture model is simply applied to the organization itself. As an institution, the organization is assumed to acquire its own patterns of conduct and learned behavior, developed within the context of the larger cultural pattern.[26]

22. A. L. Kroeber and Clyde Kluckhohn, "Culture: A Critical Review of Concepts and Definitions," quoted in Bernard Berelson and Gary A. Steiner: *Human Behavior: An Inventory of Scientific Findings* (New York: Harcourt, Brace & World, Inc., 1964), p. 643.

23. *Ibid.*, p. 644.

24. George B. Vold: *Theoretical Criminology* (New York: Oxford University Press, 1958), pp. 10–11.

25. Leslie A. White: "Culturological vs Psychological Interpretations of Human Behavior," *American Sociological Review*, December 1947, pp. 686–698.

26. Pfiffner and Sherwood, *op. cit.*, p. 252.

A third example can be cited to show that culture can act to predict behavior.

Cultural influences play an important part in determining how people will act in a certain situation. An educated European will be a better linguist than an educated American because his environment requires it. It is possible to predict with considerable accuracy that an upper class Latin-American will speak French in addition to Spanish. A carpenter will be more likely than an accountant to join a labor union. A policeman will be more likely than a school teacher to be a day sleeper. Lawyers tend to have greater verbal facility than engineers; the law exists in an environment of words, whereas engineering has a setting of mathematical symbols and graphic portrayal. Out of 100 probation workers, there are certain to be many more who believe it is possible to rehabilitate criminals than there would be among 100 policemen.[27]

---

27. Suggestions as to the philosophical role of police are given in a paper by John M. Pfiffner: "The Function of the Police in a Democratic Society," Youth Studies Center, University of Southern California, Los Angeles, 1963; also see A. C. Germann: "Community Policing: An Assessment," *Journal of Criminal Law, Criminology and Political Science*, vol. 60, no. 1, 1969, pp. 89–96; Jerome Skolnick: *Professional Police in a Free Society* (New York: National Conference of Christians and Jews, Pamphlet LC5–10/67); and Charles Reith: *British Police and the Democratic Ideal* (Oxford: Oxford University Press, 1943).

CHAPTER 3

REVIEW OF RELATED LITERATURE

REGARDLESS OF THE PHILOSOPHICAL QUESTIONS concerning *the* answer to the role of police in a democratic society, there remains the perplexing enigma concerning the lack of empirical data from which to view police organizations.

In 1901 William Lauriston Melville Lee published *A History of Police in England*. His work lacked the comparative approach which Fosdick later developed, but it gave direction and purpose to the study of police organizations.

Melville Lee described public opposition to the newly created police of London in the following excerpt:

> The formation of the new police force in the metropolis aroused the fiercest opposition and remonstrance. Invective and ridicule were heaped upon the measure from all sides. The hopeless incompetence and the discredited character of blackguardly Charlies were at once forgotten, nor were the prevalence of crime and the insecurity of life and property at all considered by those who made it their business to foment the popular antagonism.[28]

Philip John Stead, writing the introduction to the 1971 reprint edition, describes Melville Lee's work in these words:

> The present reprint, seven decades after its original, provides an opportunity for a brief account of the man who rescued police history from long neglect and mapped out the territory which others in more recent times have been able to explore.
> The main achievement of *A History of Police in England* is to have drawn in firm outline the development of the English concept of police from Saxon times to the end of the Victorian period. We cannot fault Melville Lee's understanding of the larger shape of police history. It has been accepted, often with acknowledgment,

---

28. W. L. Melville Lee: *A History of Police in England* (London: Methuen and Co., 1901), p. 245.

sometimes, regrettably, without, by those who have written on
police matters since his book was published.[29]

In addition, Charles Reith has described the contribution of
Melville Lee by stating:

> His book traces the history of the Police in England from Anglo-
> Saxon and Norman times, and through the Tudor and Stuart periods
> to the eighteenth century. It records the breakdown of the parish-
> constable system and, from their own writings, the activities of the
> Fieldings and Colquhoun. It describes the prolonged inability of
> authority to enforce laws; its helplessness and the people's sufferings
> in face of the consequences; the Police remedy which was sug-
> gested; and the fierce opposition which this encountered, causing
> long delay in its adoption. The story continues through the estab-
> lishment of the New Police, and the trials and difficulties of Rowan
> and Mayne, to a conclusion which is a brief but inspiring description
> of the Police Institution at the end of the nineteenth century. . . .[30]

A pioneer in describing the American police organization was
Raymond B. Fosdick with *American Police Systems,* published in
1920. Fosdick described his research as being ". . . based upon
personal study of the police in practically every city in the United
States with a population exceeding 100,000 and in many communities of lesser size, in all, seventy-two cities visited. . . ."[31]

Donal E. J. MacNamara in his introduction to the 1969 reprint
edition describes Fosdick's contribution in the following:

> One cannot but be amazed at Raymond Fosdick's depiction of
> American police organization, operations, and problems a half-
> century ago—for with little up-dating, both his facts and his
> strictures, his analyses and his recommendations, would duplicate
> the most recent, informed writing in the field. Visiting some seventy
> of America's larger municipal police departments in the years 1915
> to 1917 and drawing on the research that went into his earlier work
> (*European Police Systems,* 1915), Fosdick noted political interfer-
> ence, public apathy (and in fact sympathy with the criminal),
> judicial irresponsibility, too short tenure for police administrators,
> lack of proper selection criteria and inadequate training for recruits,
> corruption, unenforceable sumptuary laws, a high crime rate, the
> impact of the narcotics traffic, uncoordinated police operations,

29. W. L. Melville Lee: *A History of Police in England* (Montclair, N. J.:
Patterson Smith, 1971), pp. iii–viii.
30. Charles Reith: "W. L. Melville Lee," *The Police Review,* 1951, p. 634.
31. Raymond B. Fosdick: *American Police Systems* (New York: Century Co.,
1920), p. i.

and a host of other problems later to be elucidated in greater detail by August Vollmer, Bruce Smith, O. W. Wilson and more recent authorities.

Some of Fosdick's recommendations might well have been taken from the federal government's report, *The Challenge of Crime in a Free Society* (1967) and *Task Force Report: Police* (1967), e.g., lateral entry at higher than police recruit rank for administrative and specialist personnel, more attention to crime prevention (a principle of Sir Robert Peel's as early as the 1820's), greater organization and operational flexibility, and a central crime intelligence bureau to serve all of America's 40,000 police agencies (realized in part only in the late 1960's).[32]

Since Fosdick's report, police organization has undergone many changes during a half century of American political expansion, depression, World War II, inflation, and post–war military involvement. However, his 1920 descriptive police system can still be found, in part, in many of the "modern" police organizations today.

Not until Bruce Smith in 1940, with *Police Systems in the United States,* had new research been conducted on American police systems similar to that of Fosdick. However, limitations were established in the study by the subsequent increase of police forces to number approximately 40,000.[33]

Smith made studies of police organizations in Belgium, Canada, France, Germany and Great Britain, but did not incorporate this data into an inter–cultural study.

He did, however, make reference to foreign police systems in his *Police Systems in the United States.* Although Smith's primary concern was with the American police, in a discussion of local autonomy in that system he cited the British as an example:

... the police system of England and Wales, while it has made real progress towards coherence and unity, still rests upon the autonomy of the local governments. Under unusually able and far-seeing leadership within the Home Office, implemented by the investigations and appraisals conducted by His Majesty's Inspectors of Constabulary, there has been improvement in some of the weaker jurisdictions, and by the Police Act of 1946 most of

---

32. Raymond B. Fosdick: *American Police Systems* (Montclair, N. J.: Patterson Smith, 1969), pp. i–ii.
33. Bruce Smith: *Police Systems in the United States,* rev. ed. (New York: Harper and Bros., 1949), p. 25.

the smaller forces were consolidated with neighboring police establishments. Only 133 forces are retained in the service of almost 500 cities, boroughs, and counties.[34]

Admittedly, such attempts at comparison are relatively rare in his study. But Smith does take on a cultural direction by stressing the interaction of public attitudes and the performance of the police, as the following statement will show:

> In the long run it will be these public attitudes which determine the strength and nature of popular controls, as well as circumstances and frequency of their application. For if the general attitude is one of trust and confidence, then lay and inexpert interference with the essential processes of law enforcement should be of rare occurrence.
>
> . . . These are the reasons why the declarations of police are not accepted at face value. When they protest that civil liberties are protected "except in emergencies," they weaken popular support in many unanticipated ways.
>
> . . . Popular distrust is not a favorable climate for the consistent development of police techniques, and when these are pushed aside in favor of short-cut procedures a lawless enforcement of the law is produced which in turn arouses new public antipathies.[35]

Charles Reith, in 1952, took up the documentation of police organization in his historical account of police in *The Blind Eye of History.* Although Reith attempted to compare the United States police in terms of historical progression, his study was of the origins of police systems and was not presented as a comparison. Reith has included in his writing of police history, these observations:

> An outstanding riddle of history is the fact that police force can be seen to have existed from earliest times until the nineteenth century without being given a name. When, at last, its existence became too obvious for it to be ignored, and the need of its separate classification from military and moral force as a means of enforcing laws was recognized, it was given, not a new, clearly distinctive name, but one that was already in use with other meanings. The word *Police* is derived from the Greek, *polis,* the citadel or government

---

34. *Ibid.*, pp. 319–322.
35. *Ibid.*, pp. 343–345. A more recent intra–cultural study which viewed police behavior in Albany, Newburg, Oakland, Syracuse, Amsterdam, Brighton, Highland Park, and Nassau County was James Q. Wilson: *Varieties of Police Behavior: The Management of Law and Order in Eight Communities* (Cambridge: Harvard University Press, 1968).

centre of the city–state. In comparatively modern times, *Police* in the English language came to mean any kind of planning for improving or ordering communal existence.

. . . I submit that all means of enforcing laws comprise physical or military force, moral force and police force, used separately or together, and that military force and moral force alone or together always fail to secure sustained observance of laws in a community unless they are provided with police force, as a medium through which they can function.[36]

Historically, little attention has been directed towards police organization as part of a general cross–cultural system. While much has been written concerning individual police systems in the United States,[37] as well as those in other countries,[38] there appears to be a dearth in the literature dealing with a *synthesis* of police organizations, seeking universals from several police systems.

INTER-CULTURAL STUDIES

Those studies which approach a general cross–cultural position in viewing police organizations were amply introduced into English literature by Raymond B. Fosdick, in 1915, with *European Police Systems*. His task was to ". . . discuss critically the essential features of the police systems of the larger European municipalities."[39] Although the face of Europe, since 1914 when Fosdick made his observations, has changed considerably with the passage

36. Charles Reith: *The Blind Eye of History*, (London: Faber and Faber, Limited, 1952), pp. 9–10.

37. Individual departmental histories such as: Augustine E. Costello: *Our Police Protectors, History of the New York Police from the Earliest Period to the Present Time* (New York, 1885); John J. Flinn and John E. Wilkie: *History of the Chicago Police from the Settlement of the Community to the Present Time* (Chicago, 1887); and more recent, E. J. Hopkins: *A Study and Survey of Municipal Police Departments of the State of New Jersey* (Trenton: New Jersey Law Enforcement Council, 1958).

38. As examples, in England, T. A. Critchley: *A History of Police in England and Wales 900–1966* (London: Constable, 1967); in Africa, W. R. Foran: *The Kenya Police 1887–1960* (London: Robert Hale, 1962); Australia, G. M. O'Brien: *The Australian Police Forces* (London: Oxford University Press, 1961); Spain, Franck Arnau: *Historia de la policia* (Barcelona: Luis de Caralt, 1966); France, Marcel LeClere: *Histoire de la police* (Paris: Presses Universitaires de France, 1964).

39. Raymond B. Fosdick: *European Police Systems* (New York: Century Co., 1915).

of two world wars and a shifting balance of power, his approach and insight were unique.

Commentary on Fosdick's study of the European police has contributed the following:

> Cross–cultural studies of government institutions and agencies, their development, their problems, and above all the manner in which they interact with other elements within their socio-economic systems are of great importance today.

> Fosdick is an admirer, although not a wholly uncritical one, of the continental police systems. He sees them as having higher standards of integrity, more flexible organizational and operational patterns, and (despite inadequacies in pay, prestige, and general education) far more effectiveness in meeting their police responsibilities than their American counterparts.

> In the Summer of 1968, I had occasion to visit Copenhagen, Stockholm, Amsterdam, Berlin, Leningrad, and Moscow. Certainly the police systems in these continental metropolitan centers have undergone many changes in the years since 1914, but the ratios of police to population are today, as in Fosdick's time, still much higher than those usually prevailing in American municipalities of similar size. Furthermore, the uniforms, insignia, rank and section of designations, and more importantly the traditions and operating techniques remain strikingly similar to the descriptions in Fosdick's monograph.[40]

Fosdick's approach in analyzing European police systems divided police organizations into two types which he describes as being ". . . readily distinguishable from one another—the English and the Continental." [41]

He describes the English organization as being

> . . . characterized by its simplicity, for it comprises merely a uniformed force and a detective division. The Continental type is complex and intricate, adapted to the variety of functions which the Continental states have committed to their police departments. The English organization is built up around the work of the men in uniform; in the Continental organization the uniformed force is but one of a number of branches, each bearing an equal relationship to the head.

> Of the two types, the English possesses the advantages that go

40. Raymond B. Fosdick: *European Police System* (Montclair, N. J.: Patterson Smith, 1969), Introduction to the Reprint Edition by Donal E. J. MacNamara, pp. i–iii.

41. Raymond B. Fosdick: *European Police Systems* (New York: Century Co., 1915), p. 140.

with simplicity. It is framed for a single purpose—to carry out one line of work. Compact, responsive, and easily controlled, it performs its functions silently and with a minimum of friction.

To an outsider, the Continental type of organization appears less successful. The centralization of miscellaneous functions in one department does not seem conducive to efficiency.[42]

Fosdick is concerned that centralization of functions in one department decreases efficiency and he attributes this to the influence of the German police organization as a model for Continental policing.

In describing the Continental police organization, Fosdick stated "If it were possible to sum up in a word one's impression . . . , it would be 'over–organization.'" [43]

He further examines the two organizational types in the context of cultural characteristics. Regardless of the organizational type being used, it appears that British and Continental communities are equally well policed.[44]

Obviously, therefore, other factors than the type of organization must bear vitally upon the police problem. National habits and characteristics and a score of other influences alter the task of the police in maintaining order. A peaceful, law–abiding population presents to the police a comparatively simple problem which even faulty administrative machinery may not seriously complicate. Or again, grave defects in the type of police organization may be balanced by the superior personnel of the force.

Indeed, intelligent commissioners and well–trained subordinates, obtaining and holding office on proper conditions, and carefully selected patrolmen, appear to be of even greater consequence than any particular variety or type of administrative machinery. Certainly in searching for the factors which make for efficiency in police work we are bound to look beyond the merely mechanical arrangement of a department.[45]

Not until 1964, with the publication of *The Policeman in the Community* by Michael Banton, did a significant cross–cultural survey take place. However, Banton's main focus was the policeman, and only indirectly the organization.

Banton made comparisons of the Scottish, British, and Amer-

---

42. *Ibid.*
43. *Ibid.*, pp. 141–142.
44. *Ibid.*, pp. 147–148.
45. *Ibid.*, p. 148.

ican police. His approach was that of a sociologist researching interpersonal relationships within a cross–cultural framework. He prefaced his investigations by stating:

> It may be advisable to emphasize once again that this is a study in occupational sociology. To study the way in which an occupation is organized is not to explain away its purpose. A police administrator faced with the task of how to allocate his men, how to ensure that they do their job and that none of the less-estimable old hands has a bad influence upon the recruits, has the same problem as a works manager, a hospital administrator, or a bishop . . . . Many investigations have demonstrated that in certain kinds of factory, the workers attempt to set their own level of production: they put pressure upon any of their number who works too little or too hard. This reaction is one that seems to us very natural and we might expect it to operate in other occupations.[46]

Beyond all the recommendations and insightful premises derived from Banton's study, the import of his research is in the use of a cross–cultural approach, his emphasis on social characteristics, and his search for universal phenomena. His cross-cultural influence is well documented in this excerpt:

> . . . every social change has its costs, economic progress no less than any other. Great Britain is in the process of sloughing off a whole range of ideas about the proper ordering of the nation's life (declining industries, railway reorganization, obsolete work patterns of every kind) and moving into a phase in which none of the new ideas is assured of more than a temporary reign. . . . In many respects our social organization is coming to resemble that of the United States and many of the problems that have appeared there may be expected in Britain.[47]

George E. Berkley has described a similar statement made by Banton in the following way:

> Although Banton wrote the above comparatively recently, the scope of his analysis has already become outdated. Social change has now become symptomatic of many democratic societies; their social structures have become a good deal looser and more flexible with resulting problems for their police.[48]

---

46. Michael Banton: *The Policeman in the Community* (New York: Basic Books, Inc., 1964), pp. xii–xiii.

47. *Ibid.*, p. 261.

48. George E. Berkley: *The Democratic Policeman* (Boston: Beacon Press, 1969), p. 15.

Also in 1964, James Cramer attempted a descriptive accounting, as the title of his publication implies, of *The World's Police.* Although there is a lack of cultural emphasis, he did present to the reader a broad range of police organizations with brief descriptions.

Cramer, in the manner of Fosdick, has divided police organizations into two types: (1) British, which included all of Great Britain and the Commonwealth; and (2) all others. Under "all others" he describes approximately seventy foreign police forces. What Cramer lacks in detail in his overly simplistic descriptions, he makes up in quantity of organizations surveyed. As an example, he describes the Danish police system in five pages. [49] He avoids cultural and socially significant data. Cramer's major contribution is his encyclopedic coverage of so vast a territory, the world's police. As a reference guide to police organization, with limited data, his effort is unique in western literature.

---

49. James Cramer: *The World's Police* (London: Cassell, 1964), pp. 275–279.

PART 2

COPENHAGEN AND LIVERPOOL: TWO DISTINCTIVE POLICE SYSTEMS

CHAPTER 4

GENERAL HISTORICAL AND CULTURAL FRAMEWORK

DENMARK, ENGLAND, AND THE UNITED STATES are interwoven with the complexities of history and culture. Denmark, in the form of Danish Vikings, contributed to the early development of England by the movement of "Colonizers from Scandinavia and the continent of Europe, . . . the Normans, a branch of the Norsemen or Scandinavian Vikings who . . . crossed to England and conquered it in 1066." [1] In turn the influence of England on seventeenth and eighteenth century America, in the form of colonizing and economic control, is undisputed.

COPENHAGEN

Geographically, Denmark is approximately 16,600 square miles in size, not including Greenland and the Faroe Islands.[2] During the eleventh century Denmark ruled England in the successive personages of King Canute the Great and King Harold Harefoot.[3] In addition, Sweden and Norway directly became subordinate to Denmark in the fourteenth century, as a great part of the rest of the European continent was also much influenced by Denmark's economic and military pressures. However, during the seventeenth century, Denmark's vast sphere of influence began to wane with the Thirty Years' War and the separation of Sweden. The

1. *Britain 1970: An Official Handbook*, Central Office of Information (London: Her Majesty's Stationery Office, 1970), p. 6.
2. *Denmark*, Press and Information Department of the Royal Danish Ministry of Foreign Affairs (Copenhagen: Danish Ministry, 1964), pp. 35–36.
3. Mette Koefoed Bjørnsen and Ludvig Ernst Bramsen (eds.): *Facts About Denmark* (Copenhagen: Politikens Forlag, 1967), pp. 3–4.

nineteenth century proved disastrous to Denmark's position as a world power. Her attempt to remain neutral during the Napoleonic Wars was unsuccessful when England attacked Copenhagen and destroyed much of the Danish fleet. Denmark responded in the form of the Seven Years' War against England, which ended in national bankruptcy and the loss of Norway. Thus Denmark entered the twentieth century with a shrinking arena of influence in continental Europe and England.

Copenhagen was first mentioned in the eleventh century as a fishing village and trading place. A castle was constructed which gave ample space for the development of the town within its walls up to the seventeenth century. In 1443 Copenhagen was made the capital of Denmark. Transportation routes followed the circular pattern of the main outer walls of the castle and became known as ring roads. With the expansion of the central area of the town outwards, additional ring roads were added which have been maintained up to the present time as main avenues for motor transportation.

In the Middle Ages Copenhagen was developing as the center for Danish government and economics. Sweden besieged the City from 1658 to 1660 and again in 1801, during the Battle of the Baltic; and then, in 1807, during the Bombardment of Copenhagen, the English were successful in destroying portions of the harbor and town.

In the first half of the nineteenth century, the city stagnated and declined, but then developed rapidly, owing to the building of railways and large industrial concerns.

In 1960, more than one-fourth of the population of Denmark lived in Copenhagen and its suburbs, and the city has retained its position of governmental and economic control over the rest of the country.

Copenhagen's population has been declining since reaching 768,105 in 1950, to 721,381 in 1960, down to 654,748 in 1968; whereas the population in all of Denmark is gradually rising.[4] The above statistics are for the city of Copenhagen and do not in-

---

4. *Statistisk Arbog for København, Frederiksberg og Gentofte Samt Omegnskommunerne 1969* (København Statistiske Kontor, 1969), p. 1.

clude the suburbs of Fredericksberg and Gentofte. Central Copenhagen is approximately thirty-three square miles in area.[5]

LIVERPOOL

As we turn to the British Isles, we should use caution when describing the geographic area which is the domain of the English, in accordance with the following statement from the Central Office of Information, London:

> Care must be taken when studying British statistics to note whether they refer to England . . . , to England and Wales (considered together for many administrative and other purposes), to Great Britain, which comprises England, Wales, and Scotland, or to Britain (the United Kingdom as a whole).[6]

Unless otherwise specified, "England" shall refer to the approximately 20,056 square miles of territory which excludes Wales and Scotland. The difficulty in defining English land holdings is due to the acquisition of various geographic areas over an extended period.

Up to the thirteenth century Liverpool[7] was a small fishing village. In 1207, King John granted Liverpool a charter, turning it into a borough. Over the years, Liverpool developed into a prominent harbor; by 1685 it had become a port for shipping men and materials to Ireland. During the sixteenth and seventeenth centuries, an outbreak of the plague caused many deaths, and in 1644 the city surrendered to Prince Rupert at the conclusion of a long siege. In 1715 the harbor was transformed into a deep water port, and transportation and commercial activity were expanded. Meanwhile, all over England the industrial revolution was drawing many people to the cities and away from rural communities. Liverpool began to expand from overseas trade with the newly acquired colonial possessions. For Liverpool the most significant area was the West Indies: apart from the usual items of commerce, including some smuggling into the Spanish colonies, Liverpool was deeply involved in the slave trade and, by 1750, had

---

5. *Ibid.*, p. 62.
6. *Britain 1970, op. cit.*, p. 1.
7. The material in this section was obtained from interviews with the Liverpool City Planning Department and from Francis J. C. Amos: *City of Liverpool: Planning Information Handbook* (London: Pyramid Press Ltd., n. d.), pp. 26–27.

replaced Bristol as the chief port in this commerce.

Labor had rarely been a problem in Liverpool. The city has always acted as the main port of entry for Irish immigrants to England. The city population grew rapidly from approximately 6,000 in 1700 to nearly 80,000 by 1800. However, the major increase in population occurred during the Victorian era: the 1901 census recorded the city as having 684,947 occupants. Squalor and overcrowding were acute, and it was the legacy of this unprecedented and largely unplanned growth which has given the city its present problems of inadequate housing and unemployment.

Liverpool [8] is approximately forty-four square miles in area. As is the case with Copenhagen, Liverpool has suffered a decline in population in recent years—from 789,000 in 1950 to 746,000 in 1960, and then to 688,000 in 1968.

See Table I for a description of population and area. Here the population decreases in Copenhagen and Liverpool may be compared. Between 1960 and 1968 there was a 9.2 per cent decrease in Copenhagen and a 7.3 per cent decrease in Liverpool. In terms of density there appeared to be, in 1968, approximately 19,840 persons per square mile in Copenhagen as compared to 15,640 persons per square mile in Liverpool.

I. Political Traits

Copenhagen

The government of Denmark is based on the Constitutional Act of 1849, amended in the Law of June 5, 1915, and later amended in 1920 and 1953.

Denmark is a constitutional monarchy in which legislative authority is shared jointly by the King and a parliament. Executive control is vested in the King, who exercises this power through his ministers. Parliament consists of two chambers composed of the elected representatives of the people. Bills passed by Parliament cannot become law until they have been signed by the King. Provision is made for the King to make laws in cases of urgency, when the Parliament is not in session. Such laws,

---

8. *Britain 1970, op. cit.*, p. 15.

TABLE I

POPULATION AND AREA

	POPULATION			AREA (square miles) 1968	Population (per square mile)
	1950	1960	1968 (estimated)		
Copenhagen	768,105	721,381	654,748	33	19,840
Liverpool	789,000	746,000	688,000	44	15,640

however, must be submitted to the Parliament when it assembles, and if not approved, cease to be in force. Normally, the King cannot make laws without the collaboration of Parliament. Membership to Parliament is obtained by popular vote.[9]

Paragraph 96 of the Danish Constitutional Act of 1849 declares that "the right of the municipalities to control their own affairs, independently under the supervision of the state, shall be established by law." [10]

Copenhagen is governed by an elected council and an executive council which is directed by a mayor (borgmester).[11] The elected council selects the mayor and the remaining ten members of the executive council.[12]

In Denmark the police are responsible to the national government. The Minister of Justice is the direct representative at the national level. A Commissioner of Police (Rigspolitichefen) is responsible to the national government for the chief constables under his direction. The Commissioner of Police is primarily responsible for indirect crime control, i.e. appointments, education and training, promotion, traffic control, and criminal records. Chief Constables are responsible directly to the Minister of Justice for crime control.

Section 55 of the Danish Constitution of 1953 made provision for the establishment of a Public Affairs Commissioner, or Ombudsman:

> Statutory provision shall be made for the appointment by the Folketing of one or two persons, who shall not be Members of the Folketing, to supervise the civil and military administration of the State.[13]

---

9. The text of the Danish Constitution is printed in English in Walter F. Dodd: *Modern Constitutions* (Chicago: University of Chicago Press, 1909), vol. I, pp. 265–281; and also see Jean Bailhache: *Denmark* (London: Vista Books, 1961).

10. Bertel Dahlgaard, "Local Government," in J. A. Lauwerys (ed.): *Scandinavian Democracy: Development of Democratic Thought and Institutions in Denmark, Norway, and Sweden* (Copenhagen: The Danish Institute, 1958), pp. 174–184.

11. John Calmann (ed.): *Western Europe: A Handbook* (London: Anthony Blond, 1967), pp. 32–33.

12. *Denmark*, Press and Information Department of the Royal Danish Ministry of Foreign Affairs (Copenhagen: Danish Ministry, 1964), p. 147.

13. The Constitutional Act of June 5, 1953, Part V, Section 55.

The Ombudsman Act was passed in 1954, and amended in 1959 and 1961. The duties of the Ombudsman are to be discharged by one person, who is to be appointed by Parliament (Folketing), which, by the way, may also remove him from office if it loses confidence in him. The Ombudsman is debarred from holding appointment in public or private concerns, establishments, or institutions without the approval of the Ombudsman Committee, members of Parliament; is pledged to secrecy in matters entrusted to his confidence; and is responsible for selecting and discharging his own staff.[14]

The Ombudsman is further responsible for overseeing the Ministries and Government employees of all grades on the national and local government, not including judges and officials of the law courts.[15]

The Ombudsman is under no obligation to investigate complaints made, and must decide in each situation whether there is a *prima facie* case for an investigation. Should a case come to his attention about which no complaint has been received, but which he thinks should be investigated, he is empowered to initiate inquiries himself.

Liverpool

The United Kingdom is a monarchical state, whose origins and traditions are to be found in the history of each of its four component parts: England, Wales, Northern Ireland and Scotland.[16] Although, in theory, the powers of the monarch are unlimited, in practice they are limited considerably. Over the centuries the powers and privileges of the monarch have, with the growth of the Parliament, been considerably reduced. The Royal Prerogative grants powers and privileges by virtue of common law. The Crown is head of the executive, an integral part of the legislature, the head of the judiciary, the commander–in–chief of all the Armed forces, and the temporal head of the established Church

---

14. Parliamentary Order of February, 1962.
15. Amendment Act of 1961 to the Constitutional Act of June 5, 1953.
16. *Britain 1970: An Official Handbook*, Central Office of Information (London: Her Majesty's Stationery Office, 1970), p. 24; also see R. J. Barnes: *Central Government in Britain* (London: Butterworth & Co., 1965); and Ivor Jennings: *The British Constitution*, 5th ed. (London: Cambridge University Press, 1966).

of England.[17] The constitution is formed in part by statute, common law, and traditional practices. The rules of the constitution have never been codified; principles and practices are changeable. The rules of the constitution can be adapted to changing conditions merely by the passing of an Act of Parliament.

Parliament is divided into the House of Lords and the House of Commons, and is representative of all of the countries in the United Kingdom.

Local government [18] is divided into counties and county boroughs. The city of Liverpool is divided into wards, and representation is performed by an elected council. The chairman of the council is the Lord Mayor. The council is then divided into committees which are responsible for certain functions of the city, i.e. finance committee, works committee, watch committee, etc. The latter is responsible for the police. The power position of local government is generally described as the "local authority." Parliament has established the limitation of power to the local authority. While most powers are given to the local authority by Parliamentary Acts, special privileges can be granted to local authority by application to Parliament.

The Watch Committee is a statutory committee, appointed by the council of a County or borough exercising police functions, by virtue of the Municipal Corporations Act of 1882. Section 190 from the Municipal Corporations Act (1882) states: "The Council shall from time to time appoint for such time as they think fit, a sufficient number not exceeding one third of their own body, who with the Mayor, shall be the Watch Committee." Powers and duties of the committee shall be: to appoint constables and to establish police duties, discipline, pay and allowances, and promotion.

At the national level the Secretary of State, who is the political head of the Home Office, is responsible for public safety. In effect, the Home Office is concerned with the maintenance of the "Queen's Peace." The Home Secretary is very closely concerned with the police. He is the Police Authority for the Metropolitan Police Force and exercises indirect authority for the Police Forces

17. John Calmann, *op. cit.*, p. 83.
18. Section I, Part I, of the Local Government Act, 1933.

of England and Wales. Therefore, according to this Act, the police function is a responsibility shared by the Watch Committee and the Home Office.[19]

Revision took place in the form of the Police Act of 1964, in that the following provisions were established:

> . . . the Police Authority for a police area consisting of a County or a County Borough shall be a committee of the council known in a county as the Police Committee and in a County Borough as the Watch Committee (A Police Authority for a Combined Area is a body corporate and is *not*, unless the constituent councils concerned so desire, a committee of one of the constituent councils).
>
> The Police Committee in a County and the Watch Committee in a Borough consist of *such number of persons as may be determined by the council*, and, of that number two-thirds are members of the council, appointed by the council and one-third magistrates appointed by the magistrates for the borough or county petty sessional area from amongst their own number, in accordance with 'The Police Authorities (Appointment of Magistrates) Rules, 1964.'
>
> It should be noted that although the Police Committee and Watch Committee are committees of the council, the powers of these committees as police authorities are exercised by them in their own behalf and *are not* powers delegated to them by the council. The acts of these committees, therefore, *do not* need confirmation by the council and *cannot* be overridden by the council *except* in relation to *finance*, as Section 8 (4) of the Police Act, 1964 enacts that no sums shall be paid out of the police fund without the approval of the council. (Subject to exception in relation to pay, allowances, etc., which must be paid in accordance with Regulations).[20]

II. Legal Characteristics

Copenhagen [21]

Danish law is founded neither on Roman nor on common law

---

19. J. Conlin: *Local and Central Government: Police Administration* (London: Cassell, 1959).

20. Section 2 of the Police Act, 1964.

21. Material was developed in large part from the following sources: *Denmark: An Official Handbook, op. cit.*, pp. 205–211; the introduction by Knud Waaben in *The Danish Criminal Code* (Copenhagen: G.E.C. Gad Publishers, 1958), pp. 7–11; *The Penal System of Denmark*, Ministry of Justice, Prison Department (Copenhagen: Danish Ministry, 1968), pp. 4–6; and Johs. Andeanaes, "The Legal Framework," in Nils Christie (ed.): *Scandinavian Studies in Criminology: Aspects of Social Control in Welfare States* (London: Tavistock Publications, 1967), vol. 2, pp. 9–17.

but derives from sources that are peculiarly Danish. National legislation based on written laws can be traced back to about the year 1200.

The first Criminal Code goes back to 1866. The present Criminal Code dates back to April 15, 1930, but became operative on January 1, 1933. It has since been amended several times, the latest being in 1967. It is divided into a General Part, dealing with the general principles of liability, attempts, complicity, the system of penalties and other measures, and a Special Part comprising a selection of crimes which corresponds with the range of offenses indictable in English Law. The code is based entirely on statutes; there is no case law (see Appendix A).

The Criminal Code is primarily concerned with those types of offenses which are of such gravity as to make it natural to characterize them as crimes: offenses against the State and the public authorities, offenses against property, forgery, arson, and offenses of violence against the person. The Criminal Code of 1930 abolished capital punishment.

It is difficult to make a clear distinction between crimes and petty offenses. A distinction which is all but analogous with that between petty offenses and major misdemeanors and felonies might be found in the distinction between offenses constituting police cases, which were the former, and offenses being tried as prosecution cases before the court, the latter.

In police cases the local chief of police will prosecute, and the cases are heard in the lower court. This form of legal action is taken when no penalty other than a fine or modified form of imprisonment can be inflicted.

In most cases the decision to prosecute is made by the local public prosecutor. Preliminary inquiry is carried out under the authority of the chief of police.

Persons arrested for a crime must be arraigned within twenty-four hours. An arrestee is not obliged to give statements, and if he gives a false statement he is not punishable, regardless of whether the statement is given to the police or to the court. The prosecutor must prove that the accused is guilty and a reasonable doubt will be taken to the benefit of the accused.

Police are responsible for obtaining information and statements in connection with divorce cases and separations and cases regarding adoption, change of name, fixing of alimony, decisions regarding custody, and approval of marriage settlements.

In addition to the Criminal Code,[22] the more important laws containing rules of punitive measure are the police regulations (municipal ordinances), traffic regulations, commerce, customs, duties and taxation. Failure to observe these laws may involve up to two years of imprisonment.

The highest legal authority is the Supreme Court, which consists of a president and fifteen judges and sits in Copenhagen. The Supreme Court functions only as a court of appeal. It has jurisdiction in civil, criminal, and administrative cases. Next in authority are two high courts. These courts hold assizes in various centers within the area of their jurisdiction. At least three judges must sit in a case tried by the high court. Finally, there are just over one hundred lower courts, each of which functions within a judicial district. Only one professional judge tries each case. Minor actions are heard in the lower courts from which there is appeal to the high court. More serious offenses are referred to, in the first instance, the high court, from which there

22. See, for example, N. V. Boeg: *Danish and Norwegian Law: A General Survey* (Copenhagen: Danish Committee of Comparative Law, 1963); Lester B. Orfield: "Danish Law," *Miami Law Quarterly*, vol. 5 (1950/51), pp. 1–39, 197–237; and Hans Munch–Petersen: "Main Features of Scandinavian Law," *Law Quarterly Review*, vol. 43 (1927), pp. 366–377.

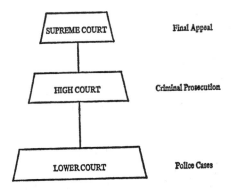

Figure 1. Organization of the Danish Court System. Path of appeals moves from the lower court to the high court to the Supreme Court, 1969.

is appeal to the Supreme Court. There is no appeal against the Supreme Court. See Figure 1 for judicial hierarchy.

Criminal cases which may involve sentences of eight years or more must be tried by the high court, formed by three judges assisted by twelve jurymen. The jury decides whether the accused person is guilty of the offense and if they find the defendant not guilty, their decision is final. Judges may, however, overrule the jury verdict of guilty. If the defendant is found guilty, the sentence is fixed by the jury and judge jointly.

Every citizen is equal before the law.[23] The Constitution declares that there shall be liberty of speech and of the press, but authors, publishers and printers are responsible to the law courts for their productions. People may assemble unarmed and hold meetings in public places, but the police may prohibit such gatherings if it is considered that they endanger the public peace.

Liverpool [24]

Criminal law in England

> . . . dates back to the twelfth century, and although in the intervening centuries there have been many changes, they have come in the course of a continuous process of development . . . . There has never been in England any doctrine of the separation of powers. The Crown is the foundation of justice, and the origin of all justice in the will of the executive that justice be done.[25]

A feature common to all the systems of law in the United Kingdom is that there is no complete code. The sources of law in all the systems include statute and unwritten or common law. Police are mainly concerned with that part of statute law which relates to criminal law and offenses which may be dealt with in magistrates' and higher courts. There is no Minister of Justice in England. The Crown is the titular head of the judiciary.

---

23. See Lester B. Orfield: "A Survey of Scandinavian Legal Philosophy," *Wisconsin Law Review*, 1956, pp. 448–480, 585–624.
24. Material was developed in large part from the following sources: Cecil C. H. Moriarty: *Police Procedure and Administration* (London: Butterworth & Co., Ltd., 1955), pp. 95–136, 163–173; Patrick Devlin: *The Criminal Prosecution in England* (New Haven: Yale University Press, 1958), pp. 106–136; Delmar Karlen et al.: *Anglo–American Criminal Justice* (Oxford: Oxford University Press, 1967); and *Britain 1970, op. cit.*, pp. 78–82.
25. Patrick Devlin, *op. cit.*, pp. 1–3.

Common law is founded on custom and supported by judgments in the higher courts. Some offenses against the common law, however, have been made offenses punishable by statute, among them, theft, murder, manslaughter, breach of the peace, and riot, to name a few. A supplementary system of law, known as equity, came into being during the Middle Ages to provide and enforce better protection for existing legal rights. It was administered by a separate court and later became a separate body of legal rules. In 1873 the courts of equity were fused with the courts of common law, so that all courts now apply both systems but, where they conflict, equity prevails.

A distinction is made between the criminal law and the civil law. Criminal law is concerned with wrongs against the community as a whole, while civil law is concerned with the rights, duties, and obligations of individuals.

The courts of criminal jurisdiction in England include: magistrates' courts, which try the less serious offenses; courts of quarter sessions, which try most of the more serious offenses; and courts of assize, which include the Crown Court in Liverpool and which try the very serious or difficult cases. Refer to Figure 2 for these relationships.[26] Trial by jury is the rule at quarter sessions and assizes.

Based on the Magistrates' Courts Act[27] of 1952, most magistrates' courts consist of two to seven lay magistrates, known as justices of the peace, whose function is to hear and determine charges against people accused of summary offenses, i.e. offenses that may legally be disposed of by the justices without a jury. In addition, they may also try certain offenses which would normally be tried on indictment, if the accused consent to forgo their right to trial by jury. Magistrates may also sit as examining justices to conduct preliminary inquiries to determine whether there is sufficient evidence to justify the committal of the accused

---

26. For general descriptions of English court systems, see F. T. Giles: *The Magistrates' Courts* (London: Stevens and Son, 1963); E. Anthony and J. D. Berryman: *Magistrate's Court Guide* (London: Butterworth & Co., Ltd., 1966); P. Archer: *The Queen's Courts*, 2nd ed. (Harmondsworth: Penguin Books, Ltd., 1963); Charles Austin Beard: *The Office of Justice of the Peace in England* (New York, Burt Franklin, 1904).
27. Cf. Courts Act, 1971. See also footnote no. 29.

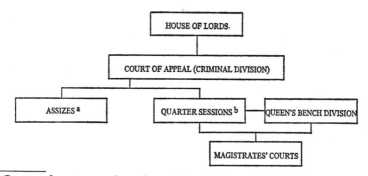

a. Courts of assize are branches of the high court presided over by high court judges and held at assize towns which are generally the principal town of each county and at certain of the other larger towns and cities.
b. Held four times a year.

Figure 2. Organization of the English Court System. Path of appeals moves from magistrates' court to the House of Lords, 1969.

for trial in a higher court. The services of magistrates are unpaid and legal qualifications are not required. A stipendiary magistrate is a barrister–at–law or solicitor (attorney) of not less than seven years standing, who is appointed by the Crown to certain magistrates' courts and is paid to perform this function. One stipendiary magistrate has the powers of a bench of magistrates. The lay magistrate is assisted by a magistrates' clerk, who is his legal advisor and the executive officer for the court.

Appeals may be brought on a point of law, by either the prosecutor or the defendant, directly from the magistrates' court to the high court. The more usual type of appeal is that of a convicted person against his conviction or his sentence, which is heard by quarter sessions.[28]

Appeals against convictions or sentences by quarter sessions, assizes or Crown Courts go to the Court of Appeal, Criminal Division. The Lord Chief Justice of Appeal presides in the Criminal Division and Queen's Bench judges sit with Lords Chief Justice of Appeal. A further appeal from the Court of Appeal to the House of Lords can be brought if the court certifies that a

28. See H. G. Hanbury: *English Courts of Law,* 4th ed. (Oxford: Oxford University Press, 1967); and R. M. Jackson: *The Machinery of Justice in England,* 5th ed. (Cambridge: Cambridge University Press, 1967).

point of law of general public importance is involved, and it appears to the court or the House of Lords that the point is one that ought to be considered by the House.[29]

Most prosecutions in England are initiated and conducted by the police. In some cases, the consent of the Attorney General or the Director of Public Prosecutions or, less frequently, of a government department is required. The Director of Public Prosecutions is also concerned with prosecutions in all the more serious cases of indictable offenses; in courts where a substantial number of cases with which he is concerned are tried, standing counsel are appointed by the Attorney General to appear on his behalf.

Criminal law in Britain presumes the innocence of the accused until his guilt has been proven. In a verdict of not guilty in a case of jury trial, the prosecution has no right of appeal and the defendant cannot be tried again for the same offense.

III. Copenhagen: Organization of the Police

A Danish police system was first mentioned in 1224 in the Copenhagen Town Regulations of that year, which describe the duties of watchmen in the following way:

> . . . it is ordained that the watchmen shall be at their posts and ready to begin their duties as soon as the watchmen's bell is rung in the evening.[30]

---

29. A restructuring of the higher courts of England and Wales was proposed by the Royal Commission on Assizes and Quarter Sessions in September, 1969. Legislative action established the Courts Act in 1971, which became effective January 1, 1972. The Act indicates that the Supreme Court will consist of the Court of Appeal and the High Court, together with the Crown Court. The High Court will deal with civil work only and the Crown court with criminal work only. All proceedings on indictment will be brought before the Crown Court. Either court may sit anywhere in England or Wales and the *courts of assize and quarter sessions are abolished.*
For a review of the court reorganization see the following: Gordon Borrie: "The Courts Act 1971—I," *New Law Journal*, June 3, 1971, pp. 474–476, and Gordon Borrie: "The Courts Act 1971—II," *New Law Journal*, June 10, 1971, pp. 505–506.
30. Valdemar H. Mensen: "The Danish Police Force," *Police Journal*, vol. 1, 1928, p. 240; also see Chapter 1 of the Danish Police School Training Syllabus dealing with police history and organization, written in Danish by J. H. Hasselriis, "Politiets historie og opbygning," September 1967, pp. 1–11.

Detailed instruction was given as to their duties and responsibilities.

It appears that the first policing was on a rotation basis by the local citizens. However, around 1590 a permanent corps of policemen was established in Copenhagen with 140 men; and in the Copenhagen Town Laws of 1643, detailed instruction was given indicating duties and responsibilities.

The police concept was firmly established by 1665 along present contemporary understanding of what the police do when a policeman ". . . was appointed for the town of Copenhagen, whose duty it was to deal with vagabonds and beggars. . . ." [31]

In 1682 a chief constable was appointed to supervise the work of the police, and it was stated in the Danish Law of 1683 that the police authority in the towns should be the responsibility of the mayor and town council. The concept of police responsibility and the administration of justice continued with the additional duties being given to the chief constable, which include the following:

> . . . the police not only had charge of the general security, etc., but amongst their other multifarious duties they had to inspect inns, enforce good behavior at public amusements, prevent loose public morals, keep the streets clean, prevent the sale of injurious foodstuffs, combat the spread of infectious diseases, supervise the quarantine services, cases of veneral diseases, and the medical service, exercise a general control of the food supply, help in case of fire, and see that the regulations with regard to extravagance in dress, food and drink, as well as those affecting games of chance and usury, were properly observed.[32]

The chief constable was authorized to appoint police constables to established districts of the city. In 1814 the chief constable of Copenhagen became *Police Director*, which still remains his title.

Reorganization of the city police took place in 1863 with the removal of the watchmen and the development of a detective bureau. Representatives of the police went abroad to study the English police system and established, in 1871, a police force which was similar to the Metropolitan Police in London.

---

31. Mensen, *op. cit.*, p. 242.
32. *Ibid.*, p. 243.

The police were reorganized again in 1919. The Act of 1919 provided for "a state police force to operate throughout the whole country, with its headquarters at Copenhagen, and under an officer known as the Chief of the State Police." [33]

The branch of government which was made responsible for the police was the Ministry of Justice. It was further required that the Chief of the State Police and his four superintendents be appointed by the Crown and that they have degrees in law. The state police were responsible for rural areas, aliens, maintaining a central identification bureau, and traffic.

It was not until 1938 that city police forces and the state police merged into one police system. The Minister of Justice became responsible for total policing in Denmark with the aid of the police commissioner and 72 local chiefs of police. The local chiefs of police are independent with regard to the administration of the police in their geographic areas. The commissioner of police is concerned with the general administrative and broad police positions of the Danish police. The local chiefs of police are concerned with the problems of regulation of life in their respective communities.[34]

At the national level the commissioner of police is assisted by twelve chief inspectors who review and supervise: the uniform force, detectives, general administration, and the national police training school. It is required that the commissioner of the police and his twelve assistants and all the local chiefs of police be graduates of law.

The Copenhagen police force [35] is headed by a Police Director and assistant directors (see Figure 3) who are each in charge of a department.

Administration Department

The first assistant is the head of all uniformed police in the

33. Hasselriis, *op. cit.*, pp. 4–5.

34. "Police du Danemark," *Revue de la Sûreté Nationale*, No. 29, 1960, pp. 3–4.

35. A more general description of the Copenhagen police can be found in the following: Kirk Viggo and Kaj Nielsen: *Politiet Arbejder* (København: Forlaget Gjellerup, 1964); and G. Sundblad: *Traek of Retsplejen* (København: Rigspolitichefen, 1967).

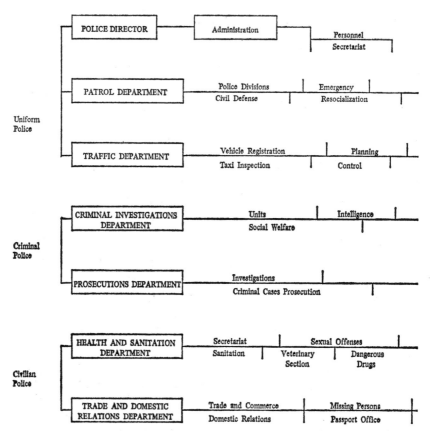

Figure 3. Relationship of the various departments of the Copenhagen City Police, September 1969.

city, and is assisted by two police commanders and 15 superintendents.

The Administration Department is divided into the following sections: (1) secretariat and (2) personnel.

The secretariat serves as a connecting link between the various sections and branches within the first department. Within the secretariat is the information office which deals with the public and press; the license office which is responsible for issuing permits to restaurants, hotels, and public performances; and the journal office which handles all the correspondence of the first department.

The personnel section is responsible for the regulation of days off, holidays, sick time, and personnel records. Disciplinary cases are dealt with by police personnel. Also within the personnel section are: a typing pool, police photographers, and a special unit of headquarters guards who are assigned to specific public gathering areas and act as guides at headquarters.

Patrol Department

The patrol area is responsible for (1) the nine police divisions, (2) emergency, (3) civil defense, and (4) resocialization as shown in Figure 4.

1. **Police divisions** in the city of Copenhagen are divided into nine geographic areas. There is a substation located in each of these geographic areas. Within the divisions are established three types of uniform patrol: point duty, where the policeman is to regulate traffic at one particular location; rigid beats, where the policeman follows a fixed route; and flexible beats, in which the policeman is responsible for a given area but is not required to follow a fixed route.

Patrol personnel are generally assigned to one of the following

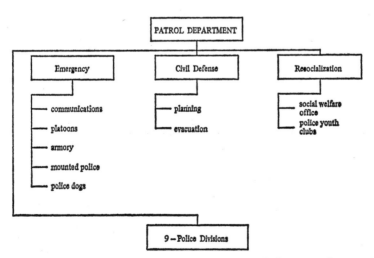

Figure 4. Organization of the Patrol Department of the Copenhagen City Police, September 1969.

tours of duty: 7 a.m. to 3 p.m., 3 p.m. to 11 p.m., and 11 p.m. to
7 a.m. Each tour of duty is worked for a full week in rotation.

Table II portrays an example of a walking beat patrol. Three
policemen (A, B, and C) cover two beat positions, and station
duty. Officer C is the relief man for both beats. Suppose A covers
this schedule (Beat I, then the Station, and Beat I again) the
first day. On the following day, B covers his beat and the Station
during the same time periods as A on the previous day. Consequently C covers beat I on the first day. It can be seen from
the foregoing, that two or three hours are spent by each beat
policeman during the day–time tour of duty at the station. The
time spent at the station is intended for report writing, assisting
in station details, and rest. At night four hours are spent by each
policeman at the station.

2. **The emergency section** is responsible for the planning and
supervising of royal receptions, demonstrations, and any large
meeting. There are approximately 185 men assigned to this section. Personnel are selected from all units of the police department. Policemen normally do not stay more than one year in
the emergency section. The personnel are divided into five
platoons: morning shift, afternoon shift, night shift, supplementary shift, and training shift. The platoons on morning, afternoon,
and night duty are divided into two groups—one of which is
assigned to patrol duty in vehicles, the other being held in reserve
so that geographic police substations might call upon them in the
event of disturbances. The supplementary platoon is prepared
for crowd control when the demand for properly equipped per-

TABLE II

DISTRIBUTION OF POLICEMEN ON TWO WALKING BEATS: DAY

Constable	Beat I	Beat II	Station
A	7 a.m. – 10 a.m. 12 noon – 3 p.m.		10 a.m. – 12 noon
B		9 a.m. – 12 noon 1 p.m. – 3 p.m.	7 a.m. – 9 a.m. 12 noon – 1 p.m.
C	10 a.m. – 12 noon	7 a.m. – 9 a.m. 12 noon – 1 p.m.	9 a.m. – 10 a.m. 1 p.m. – 3 p.m.

sonnel is immediate. With the emergency section is the command–and–control center of the force. Under normal conditions it functions as a communications system for the police force. During emergencies, control and command are centralized in this section. The mounted unit of 16 horses and a dog unit of 32 dogs are administered by the emergency section.

3. **The civil defense section** is concerned with the planning and direction of safety procedures in the event of war.

4. **The resocialization section** is responsible for preventive social work activity (often called rehabilitation). The emphasis of this section is placed in helping unemployed and homeless men who have been arrested for minor offenses. However, it is not necessary to be arrested, for many persons are referrals from other institutions to the police. The police refer to the recipient of this type of action as a "client." The police perform a thorough review of the individual's social and financial position, and, on the basis of the findings, direct the client to the proper area for improvement. Possibilities for direction might include one or all of the following: assistance in finding work, obtaining medical or psychological treatment, placement in a home for inebriates, or referral to relatives for assistance.

The resocialization section is also involved as a welfare office for community members who have the desire and ability to work but find it difficult to manage their own financial affairs. The police will assist in the administration of the client's salary to pay off existing debts and develop a firm economic base for him. The philosophy in this section appears to be a pure form of "prevention." The police feel that financial difficulties and social despair may lead to criminal activity of severe consequences.

In addition to the above work, the resocialization section is responsible for the support and administration of police youth clubs. The first such club was begun in February, 1952. The clubs are for youths between eight and seventeen years of age. The activities of the various clubs are directed by policemen with the assistance of persons in education, psychology, and the practical vocations. The youth may freely join the clubs or be instructed to do so by the courts or other public institutions. The administration of these clubs is closely associated with the local Children's Welfare Board, the Board of Education, and other public and private institutions.

Criminal Investigation Department

This department (see Figure 5) deals with all cases of a criminal nature. The Criminal Investigation Department (C.I.D.) is located at police headquarters, but also has officers assigned to substations in the city. A certain specialization has been carried into effect, for the purpose of which special units have been established.

Unit A deals with homicide, rape, assault, and blackmail.

Unit B deals with forgery, embezzlement, fraud, breach of

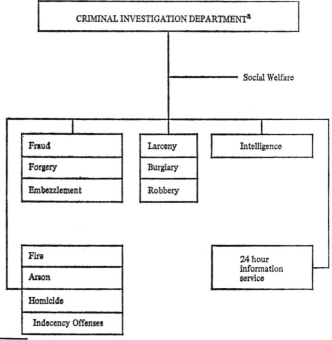

a. The Criminal Investigation Department is at the police substations between 8 a. m. and 11 p. m. After 11 p. m. C. I. D. cases must be referred to police headquarters for personnel assistance.

Figure 5. Organization of the Criminal Investigation Department of the Copenhagen City Police, September 1969.

trust, usury, debtor's fraud, perjury, and cases in connection with postal and railway services.

Unit C is concerned with burglary, robbery, auto theft, and smuggling. Furthermore, searches for wanted criminals are con-ducted by this unit, and indictable offenses are forwarded from other police jurisdictions and processed within the unit. This unit is also responsible for consultative services and educational pro-grams aimed at preventing burglary. This service is available to private persons, firms, and public institutions.

Unit D deals with intelligence collection and crimes of a political nature, such as sabotage or espionage, and carries out control of arms, ammunition, and explosives.

Unit E is an emergency group with a twenty-four hour service. Outside ordinary office hours, it receives information from the public relating to criminal information. If occasion should arise, it can supply extra personnel to the Criminal Investigation De-partment for the divisional substations.

The second department is also concerned with social preventive work. The C.I.D. feels that it is unsatisfactory to release persons who have no employment or means of subsistence, without being in a position to give them some kind of social aid.

Since April 1950, a welfare officer with certification from a school of social welfare has been attached to the C.I.D. Since 1954, however, the welfare officer has been placed at the disposal of the C.I.D. by the Danish Social Welfare Society which pays his salary. The assistance and guidance offered by the welfare officer are available only to criminals who want to consult him. His responsibility consists in developing relationships between the criminal and public and private institutions.

Traffic Department

Here the personnel deal exclusively with traffic problems. The department assists the road authorities regarding technical ques-tions, i.e. parking and traffic regulations and controls (see Figure 6). All traffic reports are forwarded to this department.

The traffic section is concerned with all aspects of vehicular safety and supervision: licensing, vehicle registration, taxi in-spection, and general safety educational programs for the public.

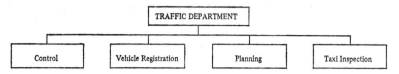

Figure 6. Organization of the Traffic Department of the Copenhagen City Police, September 1969.

Prosecution Department

This department (see Figure 7) is concerned with police prosecutions. The cases are handed over from the criminal investigation department when an accused has been imprisoned, or when statements or investigation have proven the general cause, and the case is brought to court.[36]

Figure 7. Organization of the Prosecution Department of the Copenhagen City Police, September 1969.

Health and Sanitation Department

The sanitary section conducts examinations with regard to sanitary deficiencies in residential houses, workshops, factories, and all public enterprises where food is dispensed, stored, or transported. This section maintains close inspection of all premises to be used as licensed premises, i.e. restaurants and hotels (see Figure 8).

The section for sexual offenses is responsible for the supervision of prostitutes, and deals with cases of pimping and procuring. All cases of venereal disease are investigated by this section.

---

36. For a detailed description of the prosecution department and its relationship to the other departments see A. Chosalland: "La Police de Copenhague, Danemark: Bref tableau de son organisation technique," *Croniques Internationales de Police*, vol. 10, no. 53, pp. 35–41, 1962.

Figure 8. Organization of the Health and Sanitation Department of the Copenhagen City Police, September 1969.

The veterinary section supervises the import and export of livestock and investigates all cases of cruelty to animals.

A special branch of the health and sanitation department supervises the laws which relate to doctors, dentists, and chemists in the maintenance of their records and professional conduct (as shown in Figure 8) and is also concerned with narcotics and homosexual prostitution.

Trade and Domestic Relations Department

This department is divided into four major areas: domestic relations, regulations of trade and industry, missing persons, and passport office (see Figure 9).

Domestic relations are dealt with by two branches: (1) one dealing with cases of free legal procedure in the case of separation and divorce, marriages abroad, and paternity cases; and (2) the other branch dealing with custody, conjugal rights, adoption, and applications for permission to marry when not of age. This department (as shown in Figure 9) also undertakes investigation

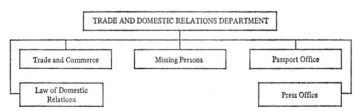

Figure 9. Organization of the Trade and Domestic Relations of the Copenhagen City Police, September 1969.

for the welfare authorities and deals with cases concerning lunatics and mentally deficient persons.

Regulations of trade and industry are maintained by police inspection, particularly in the control of weights and measures and the general enforcement of proper business practices and procedures.

The missing persons' section searches for persons who are in arrears in making compulsory contributions for the maintenance of divorced wives or illegitimate children, for persons in arrears with fines, for persons who are debtors, and for missing persons in general.

The passport section is responsible for the issue, renewal, and extension of validity of passports.

Goals

The Danish police system in principle follows the philosophy of Lepine's statement concerning the role of police, in that it is "an organized body of officers whose primary duties are the preservation of order, the security of the person and the safety of property." [37]

The Danish police organization is not oriented historically toward punitive law enforcement, but rather towards service and the maintenance of order,[38] according to Valdemar H. Mensen who was the former Commissioner of the state police.[39]

The majority of patrolmen interviewed showed greater interest in domestic relations and social work than in the enforcement of laws in a punitive way, such as by making arrests.

The uniform officers held a consensus of opinion that 85 per cent of their effort was directed toward non–law–enforcement activity. These men indicated that they perceived their role to be social rather than legalistically punitive.

Although the majority of men, patrolmen and sergeants, held the above attitude toward their work, their supervisors disagreed. Sixty per cent of the inspectors and superintendents questioned

---

37. M. Louis Lepine's, *La Police* (Extrait du "Répertoire du droit administratif," Paris, 1905), as cited in Raymond B. Fosdick: *European Police Systems* (New York: Century Co., 1915), p. 4.

38. As this relates to American police systems see James Q. Wilson: *Varieties of Police Behavior* (Cambridge: Harvard University Press, 1968).

39. Mensen, *op. cit.*

stated that the purpose of the police is enforcement of laws and, therefore, punitive. One superintendent explained his responsibility as "the elimination of the dregs from our society." Although this statement appears harsh in contrast to those of the lower ranks, it does seem to express the feeling of the supervisory personnel. Formal goals of the organization are phrased in terms of order, security, and safety of property, according to the police training syllabus.[40]

The patrol department of the police is responsible for the resocialization of persons through employment, financial assistance, housing, and aid in family affairs, in addition to interacting with youth.

At first there appeared to be a division between patrolmen and supervisors in their respective interpretation of the police role. But it was explained by spokesmen of both positions, that this disagreement is not due to organizational policy or directive, but presents two philosophical positions on Danish society. Patrolmen, the majority of whom were around twenty-nine years old, presented a more permissive opinion which has been developing in Denmark since World War II. The supervisors, older in age, many of whom were policemen prior to the War, had retained an underlying conservative nature. Many of the supervisors, for instance, described their exposure to persons arrested for the more serious offenses in these words, "It is to be expected, some people are just born bad." In comments relating to what the supervisor felt to be the goal of policing, a rather conservative and much sterner attitude was evident,[41] while the younger patrolmen revealed a far more liberal position.

In practice, however, the younger patrolmen seemed to be, in their physical and verbal approach, rigid and strict with violators of the law. This was attributed to the feeling that the formal authority of visible police work cannot be compromised, but it was pointed out that informally the patrolman has wide discretion to introduce non–punitive action.

---

40. J. H. Hasselriis: "Politiets historie og opbygning," in the Danish Police School Training Syllabus, September, 1967, pp. 1–11.

41. Reminiscent of cynicism as described by Arthur Niederhoffer: *Behind the Shield* (New York: Doubleday & Co., 1967).

In conclusion, the goals of policing, as expressed by supervisory personnel, are not universally shared on the part of the uniform patrolman. There did seem to exist a consistency of younger patrolmen displaying a style of policing which is different from that desired by their supervisors. A major difficulty for the supervisors in exerting pressure on the patrolmen appeared to be that equal recognition is given for an arrest as for resocialization of persons. Arrest or resocialization seems to be the choice which the patrolmen have to make in moving toward an attitude of protection and safety for the community.

Considering the separation of working philosophies, as we have summed them up, the trend for policing in Copenhagen seems to be order maintenance which includes non–punitive action in obtaining community protection.

Means to Reach Goals

The police organization can be divided into three parts: (1) the uniform police who are responsible for the primary police duties as well as the resocialization or non–punitive police duties, (2) the criminal police who deal with more serious crimes, prosecutions, and social welfare, and (3) the civilian police who deal with health and sanitation, trade, and domestic relations. The overall approach to maintaining community protection appears to be highly individualistic. The means seem to differ between force and guidance: force in terms of classical American police methods, and guidance in terms of permissive social welfare methods. The number of police personnel in each of the three areas are presented in Table III. It is interesting to note

TABLE III*
NUMBER OF POLICE PERSONNEL
ACCORDING TO WORK ASSIGNMENT

	Uniform Police	Criminal Police	Civilian Police	Total
1968	2,101	329	177	2,607
1967	2,024	328	185	2,537
1966	1,955	348	181	2,484
1965	1,920	342	184	2,446

* Data tabulated from Politiets Arsberetning (København: Udsendt of Rigspolitichefen, 1969), also similar reports for the years 1968, 1967, and 1966.

that the size of the criminal police and the civilian police has remained relatively stable or decreased slightly, while the uniform police has increased in size since 1965.

The police procedures utilized are characteristic of placing emphasis on the uniform police with 80 per cent of the personnel functioning in this area, the remaining 13 percent in criminal police, with just 7 per cent in civilian police. In Copenhagen there was a total of 3.98 police per 1,000 population (see Table IV for the distribution of police personnel).

The uniform police are deployed, according to geographic areas of the city, on walking beats and patrol car beats. The policemen working the walking beat do not carry a gun. As we observed them, the policemen did, however, carry a rubber truncheon which could be used, if necessary, for self–defense.

The patrol cars have two and possibly three policemen while on routine patrol. Personnel working from the patrol car will each carry a Browning automatic, 7.65 mm pistol. However 80.9 per cent of the policemen observed indicated a reluctance or indifference to the gun when asked if they thought the gun was necessary to perform their job. Policemen do not wear a holster in which the weapon might be carried. Therefore, it is necessary for the policemen to place the weapon in an empty pocket, either in his jacket or trousers. On several occasions, it was observed in the locker room, that the policeman was in a hurry to complete his dressing and, when unable to find an empty pocket for the

TABLE IV[a]

COPENHAGEN POLICE PER THOUSAND POPULATION: 1968

Uniform	3.22
Criminal	.50
Civil	.26
Total	3.98
	0 1 2 3 4

[a] Data calculated from *Politiets Arsberetning* (København: Udsendt of Rigspolitichefen, 1969), p. 4.

weapon, left it behind in his locker. One policeman stated that he removed the cartridge clip from his weapon when he carried it into the patrol car. There is a strong feeling among some policemen that the weapon is not really necessary because the men are trained in self–defense and they feel the job is not that dangerous.

One policeman expressed the general opinion this way: "Police work is different in Denmark as compared to the United States, because we don't have the gangsterism and violence. I feel no need to carry a gun."

Each patrol car is equipped with police frequency radio, rotating emergency light, and siren. Most of the time, when an arrest is made, a specially equipped enclosed van will be dispatched to receive the arrested person.

The walking beat patrolmen, as indicated in Table II, are on a rotation schedule, spending approximately three hours at the police station on relief duty. These patrolmen do not carry portable radios, but use police call boxes for communicating with the station.

All uniform patrolmen are on a rotating tour of duty, working seven days on the day assignment, seven days on the night assignment, and then seven days on the morning assignment, followed by a return to days. The patrolman receives one day off per week for rest and can be called back to duty if necessary; he gets three weeks holiday per year up to age fifty. The patrolmen seem to like the changing work assignment in that, in this way, they all have an equal opportunity to work days, regardless of individual seniority. It was stated also that the patrolman's family enjoyed the rotation because the wives could determine social engagements in advance.

Many of the uniform police indicated the rotating shift assignment afforded them the opportunity to socialize with non–policemen to a greater degree. Most of the policemen indicated no preference for policemen as family friends as opposed to non–policemen. Policemen with five years or less in the police department often expressed a preference for social interaction with others, rather than with fellow workers. Whereas, at the sergeant level and above, there seemed to be an equal division of police and non–police for social interaction.

While on patrol duty the police talked freely of increasing crime in the city and especially of the influx of narcotics which they stated were being transported into Denmark from Sweden. During these conversations it was never implied that the individual policeman should have greater technical or legal power to cope with the problem. As expressed by police on the beat, the overall impression was that the problem is only temporary. The striving for efficiency in controlling crime was not apparent. A relaxed though serious attitude was indicated when the policemen discussed their work.

It was normally required that the uniform police wear their hats while in a patrol car. Many of the police refused to comply with this demand, stating that wearing them made it difficult getting in and out of a vehicle. Forty per cent of the observed field supervisors were irritated by this lack of acceptance but failed to enforce the policy. When asked about this breach of discipline, one supervisor replied: "We Danes take great pride in being individuals; it's a small matter, so I look the other way. I am an individual, too."

The feeling of individualism is a basic ingredient in the attitude of the Danish policeman and in the philosophy of the Danes in general. The policeman accepts the concept of alternatives in performing his police duties, and a certain amount of individualism in decision making is encouraged by the organization.

Costs

The budget for salaries of police personnel in Copenhagen in 1968 was approximately twelve and a half million dollars. The salary schedule for the individual policeman is a combination of the following factors: (1) annual basic salary; (2) cost of living bonus (the basic salary being adjusted automatically twice a year to the cost of living index); (3) agreement bonus (given as compensation for the increase in wages which took place by mutual consent between the trade unions and the employers' association every other year); (4) local cost of living bonus; and (5) police allowance and function bonus (for night duty, lost days off, on–call duty and overtime work). A uniform policeman with six years' experience could thus have a gross annual income of approxi-

TABLE V[a]
ANNUAL SALARY AND ALLOWANCES FOR INITIAL ENTRANCE
TO RANK, 1968

Constable	$4,410	
Sergeant	4,984	(Automatic promotion with 14 years' service)
Inspector	4,940	
Chief Inspector	5,660	
Superintendent	7,120	
Commander	8,610	
Assistant Commissioner II	9,710	
Assistant Commissioner I	11,020	
Director	13,850	

[a] Computed from Salary Schedule, Copenhagen Police Information Office, dated June, 1968.

mately 4,656 dollars. Table V shows the annual income by rank on initial appointment to that rank.

The ordinary working hours are 42½ hours a week. The shortage of police personnel has, however, made it necessary for policemen in some stations to work a 48–hour week. The difference is paid in overtime. In addition, a clothing allowance is paid, from 48 to 115 dollars per year, depending on the policeman's rank.

The policemen in the lower ranks are very much in favor of union assistance in obtaining pay benefits and salary adjustments. Moreover the administration assumes that the union input to the police system is a just and necessary ingredient for the maintenance of equitable working conditions and pay.

Model

The rank categories in the Danish police force follow the British method of identification of constable, inspector, etc. Except for the categories of sergeant and commander, most designations are non–military.

The uniform is dark blue with identifying markings of rank easily visible.

Although, to all outward appearances, the formal organization of the Danish police is military in style, and training is conducted along the military academy tradition, the organization has a tendency to view itself first as *civilians* who are given responsibility for the safety and protection of the community.

Patrolmen in the uniform area, when asked if they view their job as being "war on crime," responded in the majority with a negative reply. One policeman, with twelve years' service replied thus: "We are at war with no one. Yes, we have criminals, but I cannot describe the police as being at war with even the most desperate criminals. Being at war is such an ugly and absolute way for a police department."

Characteristics which define a military model of policing are lacking in the Copenhagen police system. The distance between supervisor and subordinate, while on the job, does not appear to be rigid, or controlled by police policy. Respect is not maintained according to rank and position, but related to the individualism of the person. Discipline is more permissive than formalized, as in the following example: a policeman, assigned to a traffic investigation car, arrived at the scene of a minor traffic accident involving an automobile and a bicycle during peak traffic conditions in the center of the city on a major thoroughfare. The policeman conducted the investigation with his coat off, sleeves rolled up, and his hat left in the patrol car. His field supervisor arrived at the scene and, observing the dress of the investigator, was apologetic because he was not in his proper attire, but indicated it was a very warm day and had sympathy for the policeman working in the heat. The supervisor took no direct action to correct the policeman during the twenty-five minutes he was at the scene of the accident. On a scale of military to civilian behavior (see Figure 10), 85.7 per cent of the patrolmen believed the police system was civilian and on a continuum moved from center to civilian behavior.

Summary of Administrative Process

Within the administrative arrangement of the police organization there appears to be strong civilian control, intermixed with

Figure 10. The general position of the Copenhagen police moves toward a civilian approach in resolving community problems.

police authority. The civilian position begins with the Minister of Justice at the apex of the hierarchy, followed by the permanent Under Secretary, and then the Director of the Copenhagen police who has been trained in law at the University. Public opinion is brought into the system through certain committees and groups which meet with the various substation police representatives and with the director of police.

The police system is centralized within the national government, but final authority is maintained by each individual police chief in the national police system and by the Copenhagen Director of police. Decision making is maintained at the local level, decentralized from the top administrative officer downward to the policeman on the beat, with the aid of formal city council committees and informal citizen groups—but always with the philosophy of individualism as a key factor.

IV. Liverpool: Organization of the Police

The New Police Act of 1829 (see Appendix B) determined the position of the police in England,[42] one that has remained relatively unchanged down to the present time. The text of the Act was directed toward the Metropolitan Police, but has been used as an example for all police systems in the United Kingdom. As stated in the police instructions, the object to be attained is the prevention of crime; in this police system, the absence of crime is considered the best proof of its efficiency. The text also affirmed:

> Every man admitted into the police force is to devote his whole time to the service; to serve and reside wherever he is appointed; to obey all lawful orders and conform to all regulations; not to take money from any person without express consent of the commissioners; at all time to appear in his complete police dress, and to pay all debts contracted by him as the commissioners shall direct.[43]

42. "New Police Act," Extract from the *Companion to the Almanac: or Yearbook of General Information for 1830*, pp. 132–138. Also see T. A. Critchley: *A History of Police in England and Wales, 900–1966* (London: Constable and Company Ltd., 1967), and Samuel G. Chapman and T. Eric St. Johnston: *The Police Heritage in England and America* (East Lansing: Institute for Community Development and Services, 1962).

43. *Ibid.*, p. 132.

Thus, according to the Act of 1829, the police constable was held responsible for the security of life and property within his beat, and for the preservation of peace and order during the time he was on duty. The constable was "to see every part of his beat, at least once in ten minutes or a quarter of an hour; and this he will be expected to do; so that any person requiring assistance, by remaining in the same spot for that length of time, must certainly meet a constable." [44]

The definition of crime was given in terms of felonies and misdemeanors, and it was emphasized that "the first duty of a constable is always to prevent the commission of a crime." [45]

Ranks were also identified as chief constable, superintendent, inspector, sergeant, and police constable; and a ratio was established of one sergeant to nine police constables for supervisory purposes. The firmness with which the constable was required to respond to public call was stated as follows: "When required to act, he will do so with decision and boldness." [46]

The remaining portions of the Act related to the law and to procedures for enforcing the law.

The Liverpool police were mentioned in the year 1727 when it was decided by the city council to expand the night watch "in view of the great enlargement of the borough and for the more effectual putting of laws into execution especially against immorality and prophaneness."[47] This night watch was responsible from sunset to sunrise for public safety and consisted of the following personnel: 1 superintendent, 16 captains, 130 watchmen, 16 patrols, and 3 keepers for a total of 166 men.

The night watch system was highly criticized in that "the mode of watching was generally bad and the men employed both in number and ability wholly insufficient for the purpose. . . ." [48]

It was not until 1835 that a properly organized day police was developed in Liverpool. The day police system was modeled

44. *Ibid.*, p. 133.
45. *Ibid.*, p. 134.
46. *Ibid.*, p. 133.
47. J. A. Picton: *Municipal Archives and Records of Liverpool 1700–1785* (Liverpool: N.P., 1886), p. 29.
48. *Third Report of the Parliamentary Committee on the Police of the Metropolis* (London: N.P., 1818), p. 26.

along the same lines, performing duties similar to those of the night watch, but was "in no way connected therewith." [49]

With the establishment of the day watch in 1835, job description titles changed for the 62 men who worked from sunrise to sunset: 1 superintendent, 9 head constables, 44 constables, 4 clerks, 1 keeper, and 3 turnkeys. There developed a strong feeling toward the night watchman as being inferior in his duties when compared to the day police constable.

However, by 1836, the Liverpool city council described both the day and the night police as ineffective and unscrupulous for "a vicious system has long existed, and that force is most inefficient and, when disbanded, few of its members will be found eligible for re–appointment." [50] It was later stated by Gilbert in an utterance which reflected a truism of this early Victorian development of policing in Liverpool:

> Oh, take one consideration with another,
> A policeman's lot is not a happy one;
> When constabulary duty's to be done,
> The policeman's lot is not a happy one! [51]

Both styles of policing were terminated in 1836, based in part on the Municipal Reform Act of 1835. With the disbanding of the two separate forces, the city government established a police Constabulary on the lines of the defunct day police but responsible to a watch committee whose membership came from the ranks of the city council. The following was an advertisement circulated to recruit personnel in 1836 for the Liverpool police:

> BOROUGH OF LIVERPOOL. Notice is hereby given that about Three Hundred Men are wanted immediately for the Day and Night Police of Liverpool. The pay will be eighteen shillings per week and the requisite Uniform Clothing.
>
> 1. Any person applying must be not less than twenty–two or more than thirty-five years of age.
> 2. Not to be under five feet seven inches in height.
> 3. To be able to read and write with facility.

---

49. T. H. Spenceley: "Police Discipline One Hundred Years Ago" (Part I), *Police Journal*, vol. 8, no. 2, April–June 1935, p. 233.

50. *Ibid.*, pp. 233–234.

51. W. S. Gilbert: *The Pirates of Penzance* (1880), Act II. See W. S. Gilbert: *Plays and Poems* (New York: Random House, 1932), p. 175–176, for the complete dialogue expressed by the Sergeant.

4. To be well recommended for good temper, sobriety, honesty, activity and intelligence by his last and preceding employer.
5. To be in good health and of a good constitution.
6. To be prepared to engage to serve as Constables for at least twelve months.
7. To be able to deposit three pounds sterling or to find sufficient security for that sum, as a guarantee for his clothes, in the event of his quitting the Police Force without giving them up.
8. Not to keep a Public house, or deal in any Exciseable Articles.[52]

The initial strength of the police in 1836 was 290 personnel. However, by 1856 this figure had risen to 886 and has continually increased.[53] At present there are 2,248 police personnel in Liverpool.[54]

Since the Police Act of 1946, which initiated a plan for amalgamating small police forces in England and Wales, a second police Act of 1964 increased the number of amalgamations and decreased the total number of police forces in England and Wales to 47. The city of Liverpool was joined with a suburb community of Bootle in 1967 which added 203 police personnel from Bootle to the total city police force.[55]

The Liverpool and Bootle police is headed by a Chief Constable and four assistant Chief Constables who are each in charge of a department (see Figure 11).

Administration Department

This department (see Figure 12) is divided into the following sections: (1) pay and stores; (2) personnel; and (3) training dogs, and mounted police.

The pay and stores unit deals with all matters relating to the responsibility toward police and civilian personnel. In addition to the normal salary and general pay benefits, this unit is responsible

---

52. T. H. Spenceley: "Police Discipline One Hundred Years Ago" (Part II) *Police Journal*, vol. 8, no. 3, July–September 1935, p. 303.
53. E. C. Midwinter: *Law and Order in Early Victorian Lancashire* (York: St. Anthony's Press, 1968), p. 42.
54. *Report of the Chief Constable to the Liverpool and Bootle Police Authority for the Year 1969* (Liverpool: Office of the Chief Constable, 1970), p. 16.
55. T. Eric St. Johnston: "The British Police Experience," *Police Journal*, vol. 42, no. 11 (Nov. 1969), pp. 486–500; and John Coatman: *Police* (London: Oxford University Press, 1959).

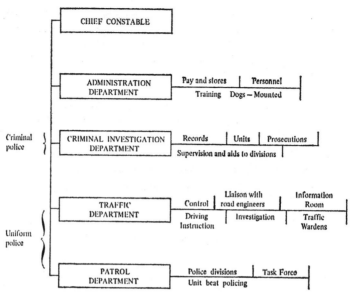

Figure 11. Relationship of the various departments of the Liverpool City Police, April 1970.

for clothing allowance and issuance, the control and maintenance of police housing or house allowance, and health benefits.

The personnel unit is responsible for the maintaining of police records and the administration of disciplinarian action. Recruitment and lecturing to civic groups, as well as public relations, have been added to this unit.

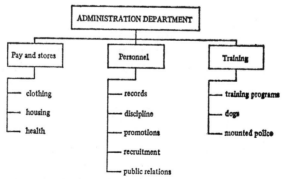

Figure 12. Organization of the adminstration dapartment of the Liverpool City Police, April 1970.

Training is divided into four stages: initial, probationer, detective, and special.

Recruits receive three months initial training at a police district training center and return to Liverpool for local procedure and elementary crime detection, which lasts an additional three weeks. The recruits are then attached to the criminal investigation department for one week and spend another week in the traffic department for field experience before being assigned to a patrol division.

Upon completion of this initial training, the young constables attend probation training on one day every month until they have completed their two–year probation.

In 1967 the Home Office approved a residential detective training school in Liverpool, which deals with criminal investigation. Two courses are offered—the initial course of ten weeks duration and a refresher course lasting three weeks. Police personnel come from all areas of England and Wales to attend these courses. The training facility has accommodations for approximately one hundred policemen for detective training.

Special training in particular areas is available for a period of between several days and several weeks duration. Some of the courses given are: man management, traffic warden, first aid, life saving, and preparation for promotions.

In addition to the above programs, the training unit is responsible for police dogs and mounted police. The police dogs are used in patrol and held in reserve for crowd control. The dogs are used principally for tracking after a crime has been committed, in searching for missing people, in searching the premises to locate criminals, and for recovering articles left at the scene of a crime, as well as in aiding ordinary police patrols. The mounted police provide assistance with crowd control and also participate in ceremonial occasions.

Criminal Investigation Department

The criminal investigation department (C.I.D.) in Liverpool consists of two main branches (see Figure 13).

The first branch consists of the detectives who are actually engaged in the daily detection and prevention of crime in the field.

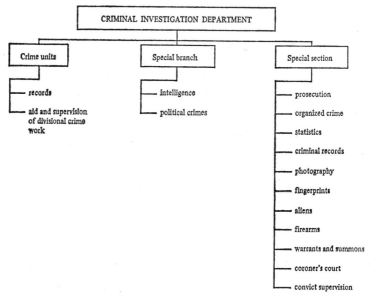

Figure 13. Organization of the criminal investigation department of the Liverpool City Police, April 1970.

Each of the seven geographic divisions of the police has attached to it a complete C.I.D. staff. In addition, there are two units: the Special Branch, which deals with outside inquiries, political matters, and intelligence; and the Special Section, dealing with major crime of an organized nature and operating all over the city from police headquarters.

The second branch, known as C.I.D. Headquarters, functions at headquarters and has units dealing with all the following special aspects of work: statistics, criminal records, photography and fingerprints, aliens, firearms, warrants and summonses, prosecutions, coroner's court, and convict supervision. Prosecutions as a police function are increasingly being placed under civilian solicitor control. Because of the need for specialization and the heavy work load, it is becoming more difficult to assign police personnel to this duty. The police remain, however, responsible for the majority of prosecutions in the magistrates' court.

Traffic Department

The traffic department operates from headquarters,[56] and has the general mission of traffic control for Liverpool. There are special units dealing with traffic planning and maintaining liaison with the city street engineers, and conducting safety programs and driving instruction for local citizens. Also, special units are responsible for traffic investigation and accident reporting, as indicated in Figure 14.

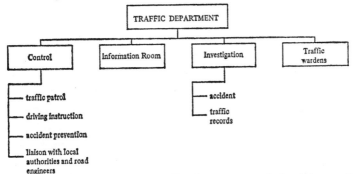

Figure 14. Organization of the traffic department of the Liverpool City Police, April 1970.

In addition the information room or central communication area has historically been associated with the traffic department since the first vehicles to be supplied with radios were used as traffic cars. Since then much of the traffic responsibility has been decentralized to the traffic wardens. The primary function of traffic wardens is to control parking violations and to function as school crossing patrols. The traffic warden position does not carry with it the same responsibility of public control as does the position of police constable.

Patrol Department

There are seven geographical police divisions, each housing a police divisional station. The primary function of these divisions is to field the patrol uniform force and the divisional C.I.D. (as shown in Figure 15).

The general patrol responsibility is carried out by policemen assigned to walking beats and motorized beats.

---

56. Refer to E. S. Wright: "Liverpool and Bootle Traffic Police: Special Problems—special measures," *Police Journal,* vol. 42, no. 2, February 1969, pp. 61–70.

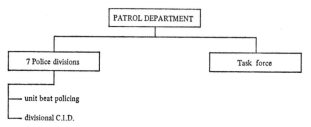

Figure 15. Organization of the patrol department of the Liverpool City Police, April 1970.

In recent years there has been an effort to better coordinate the duties of the patrol policemen. The system, which is in operation in Liverpool and in many of the other forty–six police forces in England and Wales, is called "unit beat policing." The new system offers greater flexibility of deployment of personnel and makes full use of communication techniques. The system consists of assigning policemen to regular walking beats. The area of the walking beat depends upon population, amount of crime, amount of traffic, mileage of streets, and value of property stolen. The beat constables are encouraged, where practicable, to live in the beat area or "patch." They are to develop close contact with the public so that information can be more easily obtainable. The beat patrolman will patrol on foot at his own discretion, selecting his own tour of duty—day, night, or morning. There is usually one beat patrolman per area. These resident beat policemen are supported by a police patrol car commonly referred to as a "panda" car which patrols two such beat areas in three shifts (see Table VI), twenty–four hours a day. A criminal investigation department constable is also assigned to the same area as the panda car. Contact between the beat constable, the patrol car personnel, the C.I.D. constable, and police headquarters is maintained by means of personal radio sets. With the use of the per-

TABLE VI
PATROL CAR PERSONNEL DUTY SCHEDULE

Night duty	11 p.m. to 7 a.m.
Morning duty	7 a.m. to 3 p.m.
Afternoon duty	3 p.m. to 11 p.m.

sonal radio, it is not necessary for the walking beat constable to physically report for duty at a divisional police station but only to call in over his radio, indicating he is beginning his tour of duty. A "collator" at divisional level receives, records and passes on the information sent in by patrolling constables,[57] acting as a link between units and assuming the responsibility of a command center for planning and coordinating. The collator is normally a sergeant with seniority in the police service. See Figure 16 for a diagram of the working relationships in the unit beat policing system.

The task force is a special detail composed of patrol personnel,

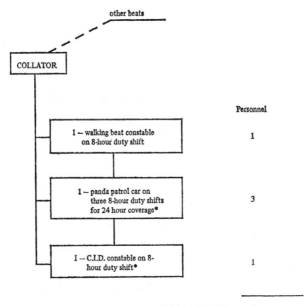

other beats

COLLATOR

Personnel

1 — walking beat constable on 8-hour duty shift — 1

1 — panda patrol car on three 8-hour duty shifts for 24 hour coverage* — 3

1 — C.I.D. constable on 8-hour duty shift* — 1

Total on one beat — 5

*Responsible for two beat areas.

Figure 16. Diagram of unit beat police system and distribution of personnel.

57. For a description of unit beat policing see E. Gregory: "Reflections on Unit Beat Policing," *Police Journal*, vol. 41, no. 1, January 1968, pp. 5–13; for general patrol see Frank Elmes: *Watch and Ward* (London: Newman Neame Take Home Books Ltd., 1965) and Central Office of Information, *The Police Service in Britain* (London: Her Majesty's Stationery Office, 1969).

working plain clothes, dealing with serious crime problems in the city. The task force is responsible to the patrol department at headquarters and follows the crime, therefore not being restricted by divisional boundaries. The main emphasis here is assisting the divisional patrol in eliminating increasing crime of a more serious nature.

Goals

Richard Mayne, one of the first of two co–commissioners of police (Charles Rowan the other) appointed by Robert Peel to implement the Metropolitan Police Act of 1829, stated that

> The primary object of an efficient police is the prevention of crime; the next that of detection and punishment of offenders if crime is committed. To these ends all the efforts of police must be directed. The protection of life and property, the preservation of public tranquility, and the absence of crime, will alone prove whether those efforts have been successful, and whether the objects for which the police were appointed have been attained.[58]

Peel's selection of an ex–soldier to enforce discipline as one commissioner and the selection of a practical and efficient lawyer as the other commissioner set the pattern for the present day police system.[59]

The concepts of protection of life and property, and of the preservation of public tranquility have come to mean, in the post–Peelian era, a division of work between the uniform police and the criminal investigation department, in that "all regular police forces have a uniform department which deals primarily with the prevention of crime and the protection of life and property, and a criminal investigation department, primarily responsible for the detection of crime and bringing offenders to justice." [60] This philosophical position concerning the means to reach the above goals is basic to all areas of police work in England.

The beat policeman (constable) performs his duties of prevention and protection in a singular fashion. The concept of the big

---

58. Sir Richard Mayne (1829) as quoted in Home Office, *Police: England and Wales, The Training of Probationary Constables* (London: Her Majesty's Stationery Office, 1969), p. 1.

59. T. A. Critchley, *op. cit.*, p. 51.

60. *The Police Service in Britain*, *op. cit.*, p. 17.

arrest seldom enters into the philosophy of the constable, either in his training or among his peer group members. However, this was not true of the C.I.D. policeman. The Criminal Investigation Department was concerned with clearance rates by apprehension; individual performance was judged, in part, by cases cleared.

Upon close observation of the police on the beat in the city of Liverpool (with its increasing crime rate), it was found that the constable, when walking his beat, remained aloof and distant toward members of the community.[61] When asked about this reserved manner, one constable replied that it was "necessary to create the proper police image." When asked what the proper police image was, he stated, "People in my community look to me for help, all types of help from fixing the kiddie's bicycle to stopping the old man from beating his wayward daughter. I can't really afford to express my own feelings; if I do, I lose their respect. And if I don't have their respect, I won't be able to count on them for help." The type of help referred to was primarily in the area of information which could be used for police intelligence. Most of the constables do not feel justified in requesting physical help, but 59.3 per cent of the constables surveyed believed the public would come to their assistance if requested.

The constable performed his protective–preventive role in the majority of contacts by nonpunitive action. The constable sees his role as being responsible for the maintenance of public order by projecting an image of public respect. In effect, he believes his major impact is in *stabilizing* the community. This position is well identified by researchers as establishing an institutional personality to develop and enforce a standard for community living.[62]

This concept of building up an image which the community can identify with in a positive way is not present in the C.I.D. The majority of detectives viewed their role as "catching crooks."

61. See Jerome H. Skolnick: *Justice Without Trial: Law Enforcement in Democratic Society* (New York: John Wiley & Sons, Inc., 1966) in his summation of the British police as being ". . . reserved, dignified, impersonal, detached. For them, the role is the man, and the example to be set is taken seriously." (p. 63) Also see Michael Banton: *The Policeman in the Community* (New York: Basic Books, Inc., 1964) pp. 188–214.

62. See Geoffrey Gorer: "Modification of National Character: The Role of the Police in England," *Journal of Social Issues*, vol. 11, no. 2 (1955) pp. 24–32.

Such American style phrases as "the fight against crime" and "crime in the streets" were heard frequently among detectives. These phrases, on the other hand, were seldom heard in the uniform–police work.

A unique position is found in the "task force" which is staffed by uniform police from the divisional patrol areas. Although required to work in civilian clothing a major part of the time, this unit is assigned to the patrol department. Personnel in the task force are ambitious in their "war on crime." Sixty per cent of the personnel surveyed described criminals as a general classification and different from law–abiding members of the community. Slang expressions, many of which were of a derogatory nature toward various ethnic groups in the community, were used to describe the suspects in cases handled by the task force.

The goals of policing in Liverpool appeared to be interpreted in various ways depending on the work tasks for which the policeman is responsible. It was stated by one constable at the patrol level that beat work is becoming more difficult "because people no longer take what we say as gospel. I mean, ten years ago I could do things that were a shade illegal. Today I have to go by the book or someone in the community will tell me where to go. I don't believe we are respected as we were once."

This feeling of losing community respect seemed to be a universal phenomenon in the beat patrol force. The constable with five years of police experience or less retained optimism concerning his relationship with the community. It appeared that constables' behavior supported Niederhoffer's hypothesis of police cynicism:

1. The degree of cynicism will increase in proportion to the length of service for the first few years, but it will tend to level off at some point between five and ten years of service.
2. Men newly appointed will show less cynicism than will recruits already in the Police Academy for some time. Recruits, in turn, will be less cynical than patrolmen with more experience.
3. Superior officers will be less cynical than patrolmen.[63]

63. Arthur Niederhoffer: *Behind the Shield* (New York: Doubleday & Co., 1967), p. 187. Also of interest is Geoffrey Gorer: *Exploring English Character* (London: Cresset Press, 1955).

Superiors—superintendent and above—who had received recognition by being promoted and were having less contact with the public, proved to be less cynical.

Means to reach goals

The police organization could be divided into two styles: (1) the uniform police and (2) the criminal police (see Table VII). It is interesting to note that the total number of police has decreased since 1967.

Whereas the primary difference in the Copenhagen police system is between force and guidance as part of individual motivations, the distinct difference in Liverpool is between force and idolatry in the person of the beat constable as projected toward members of the community.

This means of involvement at a distance, as used by the area beat constable, has a stabilizing effect upon the patrol force. Although personal appearance and a military bearing are prime tools of the constable, aggressiveness is formally and informally disapproved. There is a general feeling among the uniform police that when it does become necessary to make an apprehension, it should be done in good taste with the least bother. If the suspect were to escape, the comment would probably be, "He cannot go very far, it's just a matter of time before we nip him." Therefore, the constable goes about his job unarmed, except for the truncheon he carries with him. The majority of constables observed did not carry handcuffs. When asked about this, the general reply was, "They only escalate the opportunity for combat. I know if I were being taken in, I wouldn't like them. They create a fuss."

TABLE VII*

NUMBER OF POLICE PERSONNEL ACCORDING TO WORK ASSIGNMENT

	Uniform Police	Criminal Police	Total
1968	2,058	203	2,261
1967	2,103	208	2,311
1966	1,935	191	2,126
1965	1,947	193	2,140

* Data calculated from the Report of the Chief Constable to the Liverpool and Bootle Police Authority for the Year 1968 and similar reports for the years 1967, 1966, and 1965.

Emphasis is placed on the uniform police with approximately 90 per cent of the personnel serving patrol and traffic functions. The remaining 10 per cent are in the criminal police.

With the advent of the unit beat policing system in Liverpool, the relationship between uniform and criminal police has not appreciably changed. Although the unit beat system has been implemented, the area constable is critical of the plan. His major criticism is that more men are needed to participate in this team approach to policing, and the force in 1968 was undermanned by approximately five hundred personnel. The constables feel that unit beat policing puts unrealistic requirements on the police. They also suggest that the system does not work in a large city with a big transient population.

In actual practice, the C.I.D. police stated that they did not come into contact with the patrol car constable or area beat constable appreciably more than prior to the system. The majority of the C.I.D. work is based on citizen reports of crime and information from the collator.

Some panda car police constables felt they were being used for messenger service when they interacted with the area constable. The area constable seldom ventures to the divisional station, and any supplies or reports are generally transmitted via the panda car.

Panda cars are manned by one constable while on routine patrol. No weapons are in evidence in the car other than the ordinary truncheon which is carried by all constables. The patrol car constables are on a rotating tour of duty, working seven days on the day assignment, seven days on the night assignment, then switching to a morning assignment for seven days, and finally returning to days. Most of the constables preferred the rotating shifts of duty.

Constables receive one and three–fourths days off per week, but can be called back to duty if necessary. Police personnel are entitled to a period of annual leave. From chief inspector to constable, the periods scale down from twenty-five to seventeen days. From superintendent upwards the annual leave period is to be not less than forty-two days with an additional six days after completing ten years' service.[64]

Police constables are prohibited by police regulations from holding any other office or employment or carrying on any business for hire or gain without permission of the Chief Constable.

The pattern, established under Peel, of military discipline and protocol is very much apparent among the various ranks of police. A strong sense of military etiquette and distance is maintained between subordinate and superior. Headquarters and divisional stations maintain segregated facilities for personnel according to rank. In practice, personnel have eating areas, bar facilities, and recreational equipment on a military basis similar to the grouping of enlisted personnel, noncommissioned personnel, and officer personnel. It is evident that junior officers are subordinates when in the company of higher ranking members of the police.

When an inspector was asked about these relationships, his only reactions were a wink of the eye, a grin, and the single word of explanation—"tradition"—before ending the conversation and walking away.

The rate of police per thousand population in Liverpool is given in Table VIII. It is interesting to note that Liverpool, with a

TABLE VIII[a]
LIVERPOOL POLICE PER THOUSAND POPULATION: 1968

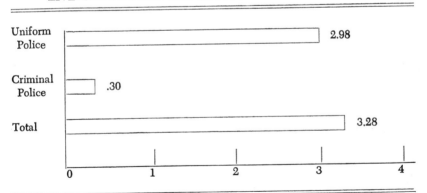

Uniform Police	2.98
Criminal Police	.30
Total	3.28

[a] Data calculated from the Report of the Chief Constable to the Liverpool and Bootle Police Authority for the Year 1968, p. 15.

64. Moriarty, *op. cit.*, pp. 242–243.

greater population in 1968 than Copenhagen, had a smaller ratio of police per thousand inhabitants. In comparing police per thousand population it was evident that Copenhagen had 3.98 police per thousand, while Liverpool had 3.28.

The majority of patrol cars are manned with one constable. The panda cars and traffic cars are equipped with emergency lights, siren, and radio. The patrol cars are smaller than the automobiles used in Copenhagen. However, prisoners are often transported in the back seat to the station. Little concern was expressed for the safety of the constable during this type of transportation, since few injuries had occurred in the past under these circumstances.

The uniform is basically the same as that worn in the Metropolitan police force. Walking beat constables wear the helmet style hat while the constables working the panda and traffic cars bear a brimmed cap which facilitates entry and exit from the car.

In Liverpool the police are allowed to purchase their own homes. There is police housing available for those who desire this type of accommodation. It is generally at the discretion of the Chief Constable if he allows his men to purchase their own housing. In the past, all police housing was provided by the police authority, so that ranks were many times clustered together and the city policemen only associated with one another during off–duty hours. Adequate housing in general is difficult to obtain in Liverpool. Demands are made by the Police Federation for policemen to select their own housing, and also the police authority believes that the economic burden is becoming too great in terms of construction and maintenance for police housing. Consequently the present trend is for rent allowances which are to be applied toward their housing.

The majority of men preferred the rent allowance and the opportunity to purchase their own home. Disadvantages existed in that promotion or transfer from the Liverpool force to another of the total forty-seven police forces in England and Wales created hardships in their attempt to dispose of a personal residence.

The policeman's family recently has had greater opportunity to socialize with non–police families. However, many policemen purchase homes in the same geographic area and still have a tendency to fraternize socially.

Costs

The budget for salaries of Liverpool police personnel in 1968 was approximately five and a half million dollars. The salary schedule for the individual policeman was a combination of the following factors: (1) rent allowance; (2) uniform, boot, and equipment allowance; (3) an undermanning allowance; and (4) overtime pay. A uniform policeman with six years' experience receives a gross annual income of approximately 2,740 dollars. Table IX reflects the gross annual income by rank on initial appointment.

TABLE IX*
ANNUAL SALARY AND ALLOWANCES
FOR INITIAL ENTRANCE TO RANK, 1968

Constable	$1,836
Sergeant	3,060
Inspector	3,600
Chief Inspector	4,040
Superintendent	4,760
Chief Superintendent	5,710
Assistant Chief Constable	10,604
Chief Constable	16,315

* Computed from salary schedule, Home Office and the Central Office of Information, *Your Career in Britain's Modern Police* (London: Her Majesty's Stationery Office, 1968), p. 12.

As already noted, ordinary working hours are forty-two hours a week with one and three-fourths days off per week. However, Liverpool is undermanned by five hundred personnel, which fact necessitates paid overtime for most constables. Since outside employment is regulated according to formal organizational policy, the majority of men look forward to working additional days for overtime pay.

Policewomen are permitted to work 10 per cent less time than their male counterparts. The women also receive 10 per cent less salary. There seemed to be a negative attitude on the part of the constable toward female police in general. Policewomen are required to perform traffic control, walking beat patrol, patrol car work, and crowd control.

Model

The Liverpool police system follows the military mode. When asked how to describe the behavior of the police, a majority of the constables indicated it was military in manner. Through the Police Federation, which is a quasi–union for police personnel in England, demands have been made of the police authority and the chief constable which are contrary to police philosophy. Most of these demands have been in the area of salary and allowances, but now some of the younger constables are requesting the use of guns which they said would have a deterring effect upon the criminal type. However, it was felt by many ranking police personnel that guns would not play as important a role in the life of the constable as it has in the American police system. Although there is agitation by some for guns, the general feeling is that the movement would not be successful.

Whereas, the Copenhagen police viewed themselves as civilians who are responsible for the safety and protection of community affairs, the Liverpool police see their role to be military in the carrying out of their police duties.

The police system is often referred to as a disciplined service.[65] On a scale of military to civilian behavior (see Figure 17 which portrays the philosophy which is expressed in the police system), the movement leans from center toward a military style of organization, in the opinion of the constables surveyed.

Figure 17. The general position of the Liverpool police leans toward a military approach in resolving community problems.

Summary of Administrative Process

The administrative process of the British police system is best described as a strong police position with a weak civilian au-

---

65. See for example *A Handbook of Police Discipline* (London: The Police Federation, 1966); and David Wiliams: *Keeping the Peace: The Police and Public Order* (London: Hutchinson & Co. Ltd., 1967).

thority. The Liverpool police assumes the position of a strong bureaucratic organization with close supervision of civilian personnel by police personnel.

There is a feeling of inferiority in civilian positions within the force. This was very much apparent when the police supervisor of twelve civilian clerks complained, "These girls are lazy. They are not dedicated to their work. If I could have three policemen, they could do the work of the whole lot. You just have to keep your eye on these clerks every minute."

The police system is similar to that of Denmark in that centralization has taken place at the national level in the area of direction and general police policy, but still final authority is maintained by each chief constable at the local level. Decision making is maintained in the local force with greater control over discipline and training than is the case with the constable in the Danish police system.

V. Personnel Development

It has been stated that "the caliber of police service is almost completely determined by personnel policy, and very largely at the intake (the start) by recruiting standards." [66] From this position, Copenhagen and Liverpool are viewed in terms of recruitment, training and promotion.

Recruitment in Copenhagen

In order to be employed as a police constable the applicant has to fulfill the following requirements: (1) be a Danish citizen, (2) complete his military service with a good record, (3) be between twenty-one and twenty-five years of age, (4) be at least 5 feet 9-½ inches tall, and (5) be in a state of good health proven by a medical certificate.

Before the person is given an application form he is subjected to an elementary test covering a written exercise in Danish and arithmetic. The test is administered in the police area in which

66. V. A. Leonard: *Police Organization and Manager*, 2nd ed. (Brooklyn: The Foundation Press, Inc., 1964), p. 90. Also see George Berkley: "The European Police: Challenge and Change," *Public Administration Review*, vol. 28 (September-October 1968), pp. 424–430.

the applicant resides. Application papers are completed and the applicant is then interviewed by the local chief constable and examined by a selection committee of four members. On the basis of a physical exercise examination, swimming test, and the opinion of the selection committee, the national commissioner of police then decides upon the applicant's appointment to the police.

No diploma or degree is required for appointment in the police. This is usually emphasized to make police personnel representative of the entire population.

Recruitment in Liverpool

Recruits must be of good character and physically fit. The Liverpool recruit may be between nineteen and thirty years of age, although former servicemen over thirty years of age may be considered. The minimum height requirement is 5 feet 8 inches. A general written entrance examination is required. The candidate is then subjected to an interview and, if successful, is sworn in and begins a two–year probationary period of training and police duties, before he becomes established as an officer of the police force.

To increase the proportion of recruits with a high educational standard, a university graduate entry scheme has been introduced. Under this plan, graduates and undergraduates in their final year at a university, who apply to join the police service, are selected by an "extended interview" which lasts for two and one half days and includes group discussion, interview, and intelligence tests. The university–trained recruit is given the opportunity for accelerated promotion (after further interview) when he has served the two–year probationary period in the normal way.

The Police Act of 1964 allows the Home Secretary to make regulations for police service:

> No person shall be eligible for appointment to a police force and the services of a member of a police force may be dispensed with at any time, if, without the consent of the Chief Officer of Police:
> (A) He carries on any business or holds any other office or employment for hire or gain, or
> (B) He resides at any premises where his wife or any member of his family keeps a shop or carries on any like business, or

(C) He holds, or his wife or any member of his family living with him holds, any license granted in pursuance of the liquor licensing laws, or the laws regulating places of public entertainment in the area of the police force in which he seeks appointment, or to which he has been appointed, as the case may be, or has any pecuniary interest in such license, or

(D) His wife, not being separated or divorced from him, keeps a shop or carries on any like business in the area of the police force in which he seeks appointment or to which he has been appointed, as the case may be.[67]

In addition, a constable serves wherever he is ordered, and his place of residence is subject to the approval of the chief constable. A constable promptly discharges all lawful debts and, in case of failure to do so, must report the circumstances to the chief constable. And a constable avoids, whether on duty or in private life, any conduct or behavior likely to bring discredit to the police service. He also abstains from any activities calculated to interfere with the impartial discharge of his duties and, in particular, he does not take any active part in politics.

Training in Copenhagen

Immediately after appointment, a Danish police constable is on probation for two years.[68] During this time he attends training schools for a total period of approximately eight months.

The first training is identified as A–course and lasts eleven weeks, forming the first part of the elementary training offered by the police. Subjects which are taught include the following: (1) Danish, (2) report writing, (3) police knowledge, (4) traffic law, (5) trade act, (6) gymnastics and self–defense, (7) typewriting, (8) shooting, (9) drawing, (10) first aid, (11) penal code, (12) family law, (13) alien act, (14) describing and object learning, (15) automotive repair, (16) criminal record and Danish police intelligence, (17) electricity, (18) civics, (19) English and/or German, (20) civil defense, and (21) driving theory and practice.

After the A–course the constable is assigned to a divisional

67. Police Act, 1964, Section 33.
68. For an earlier description of police training refer to H. S. Kemble: "The Danish State Police School," *Police Journal*, vol. 12, no. 2, April-June 1948, pp. 151–154.

station for six to nine months for practical experience. After completing this time he is reassigned to the training school for an additional twenty–two weeks of training in the B–course.

The B–course covers more intently the areas identified above. At the conclusion of the B–course, examinations are given in Danish, report writing, elementary police knowledge, traffic, trade and business legislation, physical exercises and self-defense. After successful completion of these examinations the constable returns to a field assignment. At the conclusion of two years the constable is retained if he has been successful in his training and work experience.

Before the termination of his sixth year of service the police constable attends another training course of twenty-two weeks duration to complete his elementary training. During this course, examinations are held in the following subjects: report writing, language, law of domestic relations, licensing act, penal code and administration of justice, traffic, patrol procedures, elementary police knowledge and investigation, physical exercises and self–defense, civics, social knowledge, health service, fire services act, forensic medicine, automotive repair, and duties of civil servants.

Arranging the subject areas in percentage of time devoted to each area and placed in rank order from most to least time, the following five topics take 71.2 per cent of the total course time in the Copenhagen training program.

Emphasis in Copenhagen is placed upon the teaching of language. Liverpool does not have an equivalent area in its training program.

MAIN AREAS OF THE COPENHAGEN TRAINING PROGRAM

RANK ORDER	SUBJECT AREA	PERCENTAGE
1.	Language (Danish and English and/or German)	21.0
2.	Patrol Procedures	17.0
3.	Introduction to Law Enforcement	13.7
4.	Traffic	10.0
5.	Criminal Law	9.5
	TOTAL	71.2

After having passed this course, the police constable has the possibility of being employed in the criminal investigation department or civilian police. If selected for one of these new assignments, he will have to take a detective constable's course of twelve weeks duration or a civilian police constable course for nine weeks.

After fourteen years of service the constable is automatically promoted to police sergeant or detective sergeant.

Training in Liverpool

Police training here is organized under three major categories: (1) recruit training, (2) specialized training for constables who show an aptitude for duty in some particular facet of police work, and (3) higher training at the police college to prepare officers for the most senior posts in the police force.

Recruits spend approximately thirteen weeks at a residential training center. The emphasis in the basic training course is on police duties and physical fitness. The course covers the following areas: elementary law, court procedure, crowd control, traffic control, physical training, self–defense, civil defense, first aid, swimming and life saving. Practical training and demonstrations are presented to dramatize situations which might be encountered by the constable. At the conclusion of this training the probationary constable returns to Liverpool–Bootle and is assigned to a working unit. He continues his training by attending the Liverpool training school one day per month until he completes his two-year probation. Local procedure is taught which reshapes the general training to fit the needs of Liverpool. As stated in a description of police training: "The object of these courses is to ensure that constables posted to their first station and carrying out general police duties under supervision become fully conversant with police procedure and practice, regulations and by-laws, and any problems peculiar to the district." [69] At the conclusion of fifteen months service, probationers attend a further four–week residential course as a refresher, to re-enforce the knowledge assembled at this point in their police service.

Arranging the subject areas in percentage of time devoted to each area and placed in rank order from most to least time, the

---

69. *The Police Service in Britain* (London: Her Majesty's Stationery Office, 1969), p. 25.

following five topics take 65.4 per cent of the total course time in the Liverpool training program.

MAIN AREAS OF THE LIVERPOOL TRAINING PROGRAM

RANK ORDER	SUBJECT AREA	PERCENTAGE
1.	Criminal Investigation	18.3
2.	Patrol Procedures	15.5
3.	Traffic	12.3
4.	Criminal Law	10.7
5.	Criminal Evidence	8.6
	TOTAL	65.4

Criminal investigation is stressed in the Liverpool training course with 18.3 per cent of the total time devoted to this area.

Training for specialist duties is carried out at the Liverpool training school. Courses of this type for constables include: riding and care of horses, dog handling, fingerprint classification and preparation for future detectives. Detective training is offered in junior and intermediate courses for constables. The course includes a detailed survey of criminal law as it affects the work of police officers, court procedure, the rules of evidence, and detailed information about basic types of crimes committed in Liverpool. Refer to Table X for a comparison of training topics and number of hours in training programs.

Promotion of Copenhagen Police

After fourteen years the policeman is automatically promoted to the level of sergeant, and then has the opportunity to seek higher promotion to inspector and superintendent. A higher promotion is actually decided by the commissioner of police, based upon statements given by superiors of the man seeking advancement. No further education on the part of the policeman is necessary prior to promotion. However, after obtaining the advancement the officer has to attend a management course for administrative officers.

The management courses are divided into Parts I and II. Managemont I has a duration of eleven weeks and the instruction includes the following subjects: penal code and administration of justice act, civil law, legislation on damages, psychology for leaders, police tactics, civil defense, civics, lectures and study

TABLE X
COMPARISON OF TRAINING TOPICS
AND NUMBER OF HOURS IN TRAINING PROGRAM*

TRAINING TOPIC AREA	COPENHAGEN*		LIVERPOOL**	
	Hours	Percent	Hours	Percent
1. Introduction to law enforcement (orientation, history of law enforcement, departmental policies and civics)	188	13.7	37	6.3
2. Criminal Law (criminal code law)	130	9.5	64	10.7
3. Criminal Evidence (rules of evidence)	7	.5	51	8.6
4. Administration of Justice (court system, courtroom demeanor, and testifying)	10	.7	39	7.4
5. Criminal Investigation (Investigation of specific crimes)	102	7.5	149+	18.3
6. Patrol procedures (patrol, observation, and report writing)	231	17.0	80+	15.5
7. Traffic Supervision (Traffic investigation and driving practice	138	10.0	60+	12.3
8. Juvenile Procedures (Techniques used in dealing with youth)	4	.3	18	3.1
9. Physical Conditioning	125	9.2	20	3.3
10. Defense Tactics (Physical defense)	60	4.4	27+	4.6
11. Firearms (Legal aspects and firing weapons)	35	2.6	8	1.2
12. First Aid	18	1.3	9+	3.1
13. Community Relations (Human interaction)	20	1.5	27+	4.6
14. Language: Danish English and/or German	205 80	15.1 5.9		
15. Psychology and Sociology (Personal behavior)				
16. Civil Defense (Enemy attack)	12	.8	6	1.0
TOTAL	1,365	100.0	595	100.0

* Data gathered from departmental records and observation of classroom training for Copenhagen and Liverpool, 1969.
* The topics covered are based upon 41.4 hours per week for 33 weeks for a total of 1,365 hours.
** The topics covered are based upon 35 hours per week for 17 weeks (a 13 week residential course and approximately a 4 week course at the Liverpool-Bootle training school) for a total of 595 hours.

group work. This course is finished with a written and oral test mainly in the subjects of penal code, administration of justice act, and police tactics. The results of this examination are of real importance when the question of further promotion is raised.

The Management II course is for a duration of 4½ weeks and includes instruction in supervision, planning, division of labor, judging and selection of personnel, sociology, administrative law, penal code, and administration of justice act.

Apart from the above courses the police training school also has courses for all ranks of police, to be taken every eighth year of employment as refresher courses of approximately two weeks each. In addition, special courses are available of from one to three weeks duration for administrative officers, dealing with bookkeeping and accounting, fire prevention, prevention of juvenile crimes, and intelligence service.

Promotion of Liverpool Police

Appointments to the higher ranks of the force are filled from within the police. One of the conditions for promotion to "sergeant" or "inspector" is to pass qualifying examinations in police subjects. No qualifying examinations are set for promotion to ranks above inspector. Promotion to sergeant is possible during the third year's employment. The rank of inspector can be reached in another two years, with promotion to superintendent in an additional two years.

A national qualifying examination in professional police subjects must be passed before promotion to sergeant. Those who show exceptional potential and ability in the qualifying examination might further compete for the twelve–month special course at Bramshill Police College. To qualify for it, policemen are selected on a national basis by a rigorous selection procedure based partly on their performance in the examination and partly by means of extended interviews similar to those required for entry to higher posts in British civil service. Policemen receive temporary promotion to sergeant during the course and permanent promotion upon successful completion.

Sergeants serve two years in this rank and pass an examination in police subjects before being promoted to inspector. Policemen who successfully complete the special course at Bramshill are exempt from this examination and, after satisfactorily completing a further year's employment with the rank of sergeant, will be promoted to the rank of inspector.

For promotion to ranks above inspector there are no qualifying examinations. Selection depends on merit. Higher training for police is conducted, in residence, at the Police College at Bramshill. The board of governors of the college consists of representatives of the local authority associations, the Home Office, and police personnel. The governors are assisted by an advisory committee comprised of representatives of all ranks of the police service. The directing staff of the college includes police officers from various forces throughout the country serving for a two-year period and a permanent academic staff. Speakers from various areas are invited to lecture at the college as necessary.

The four courses at the college are: (1) the senior command course for officers of higher seniority rank who have the potential to become chief constable or assistant chief constable; (2) the intermediate command course for chief inspectors and newly promoted superintendents to prepare them for their first command; (3) the inspectors' course for recently promoted inspectors, to prepare them for dealing with the problems likely to be met by officers of that rank; and (4) the special course for selected young policemen for accelerated promotion.

All these courses are residential. Their duration is from three months for the intermediate command course to a year for the special course. Policemen for the senior command and special course are selected by extended interview which lasts two and a half days. Policemen attending the other courses are nominated by the police authority or the chief constable of their respective force. General and professional studies are common to the courses taught, and increasing emphasis is being placed on management techniques, the application of science and technology to police work, and the methods of dealing with major disasters, and with such current problems as dangerous drugs and race relations.

VI. Selected Readings
Danish Police Literature

General

Boeg, N. V. *Danish and Norwegian Law: A General Survey.* Copenhagen: Danish Committee of Comparative Law, 1963.

Jacobsen, B. *Selvforsvar.* København: Borgens Forlag, 1962.

Juul, Stig, *et al. Scandinavian Legal Bibliography.* Uppsala: Acta Instituti Upsaliensis Jurisprudentiae Comparativae, 1961.

Mellerup, E. *Det gamle København pa vrangen.* København: Forlaget Fremad, 1964.

Mellerup, E. *I festlige og farlige tider.* København: Forlaget Fremad, 1957.

Sundblad, G. *Traek af retsplejen.* København: Rigspolitichefen, 1967.

Viggo, Kirk and Kaj Nielsen. *Politiet arbejder.* København: Forlaget Gjellerup, 1964.

Periodicals and Journals

Kriminalpolitibladet: Dansk Kriminalpolitiforening. Anker Heegardsgade 7, 1572. København V.

Poltibladet: Dansk Politiforbund. N. J. Fjords, Fjords Allé 8, 1957, København V.

Politiet: Tidsskrift for politivaesen. Rigspolitichefen. Anker Heegardsgade 5, 1572, København V.

English Police Literature

General

Critchley, T. A. *A History of Police in England and Wales, 900–1966.* London: Constable and Company, Ltd., 1967.

Devlin, J. Daniel. *Police Procedure, Administration and Organization.* London: Butterworths, 1966.

Lee, W. L. Melville. *A History of Police in England.* Montclair, New Jersey: Patterson Smith, 1971.

Marshall, Geoffrey. *Police and Government.* London: Methuen & Co. Ltd., 1965.

Reith, Charles. *British Police and the Democratic Ideal.* Oxford: Oxford University Press, 1943.

Home Office. *Report of Departmental Committee on Detective Work and Procedure.* (5 Volumes). London: Her Majesty's Stationery Office, 1938–39.

Home Office. *Higher Training for the Police Service in England and Wales.* (CMD. 7070). London: Her Majesty's Stationery Office, 1947.

Home Office. *Memorandum on the Design and Construction of Police Stations.* London: Her Majesty's Stationery Office, 1955.

Home Office. *The Report of Working Group in Crime Prevention Methods.* London: Her Majesty's Stationery Office, 1956.

Home Office. *Report of the Committee of the Police Council for England and Wales on Police Uniform.* London: Her Majesty's Stationery Office, 1958.

Home Office. *Police of the Metropolis.* London: Her Majesty's Stationery Office, 1960.

Home Office. *Police in Counties and Boroughs.* London: Her Majesty's Stationery Office, 1960.

Home Office. *Police Training in England and Wales.* (Cmnd. 1450). London: Her Majesty's Stationery Office, 1961.

Home Office. *Report of the Committee of the Police Council on Higher Police Training.* London: Her Majesty's Stationery Office, 1962.

Home Office, *Royal Commission on the Police Final Report.* London: Her Majesty's Stationery Office, 1962.

Home Office. *Police Dogs: Training and Care.* London: Her Majesty's Stationery Office, 1963.

Home Office. *Judges' Rules and Administrative Directions to the Police.* London: Her Majesty's Stationery Office, 1964.

Home Office. *The Police Regulations.* London: Her Majesty's Stationery Office, 1965.

Home Office. *Report of Working Party on Police Cadets.* London: Her Majesty's Stationery Office, 1965.

Home Office. *Committee on the Prevention and Detection of Crime, Part 1.* London: Her Majesty's Stationery Office, 1965.

Home Office. *The Planning of Police Buildings.* London: Her Majesty's Stationery Office, 1966.

Home Office. *Report of Working Parties on Police Manpower, Equipment and Efficiency.* London: Her Majesty's Stationery Office, 1967.

Home Office. *The Recruitment of People with Higher Educational Qualifications into the Police Service.* London: Her Majesty's Stationery Office, 1967.

Home Office. *Police Regulations.* London: Her Majesty's Stationery Office, 1968.

Periodicals and Journals

British Journal of Criminology. Stevens & Sons, 11 New Fetter Lane, London, E.C.4.

Current Law. Sweet and Maxwell Ltd., 11 New Fetter Lane, London, E.C. 4.

Forensic Science Society Journal. The Forensic Science Society, 107 Fenchurch Street, London, E.C. 3.

Police College Magazine. Police College, Bramshill House, Hartley Witney, Hampshire.

Police Journal. Butterworth & Co., Ltd., East Row, Little London, Chichester.

Police Research Bulletin. Home Office Research and Development Branch, Horseferry House, Dean Ryle Street, London, S.W. 1.

Police Review. Police Review Pub. Co., Ltd., 67 Clerkenwell Road, London.

Police World. M. & W. Publications Ltd., 19a Ashley Place, London, S.W. 1.

PART 3

DESCRIPTIVE OUTLINES OF SELECTED COMPARATIVE POLICE ORGANIZATIONS

CHAPTER 5

POLICE ORGANIZATIONAL CHARACTERISTICS

T HE FOLLOWING TEN COUNTRIES: Austria, Belgium, France, Germany (West), Italy, The Netherlands, Norway, Spain, Sweden, and Switzerland were selected to develop a wide area for comparative police systems. The descriptive analyses present a portrait of each police system. Investigations of these police organizations have synthesized direct observations, participation, and review of the literature to provide comparative cameos for inclusion in this study.[1]

Much insight can be gained regarding each police system when placed in a particular cultural setting of political traits, legal characteristics and organization of the police.

I. AUSTRIA

Political Traits

Austria has a land area of approximately 33,000 square miles with a population of about seven and a half million people.

Austria is a democratic federal republic. It is divided into nine states (Länder) with individual constitutions and municipal governments.

A president is elected by popular vote for a term of six years. The president holds executive power, commands the military, represents the government abroad, and appoints other members of the national government.

---

1. At the conclusion of each section (dealing with one of the countries just named) in this chapter, a list of "Selected Readings" is provided for further information for the interested reader.

The national government consists of a chancellor, a vice–chancellor, ministers, and secretaries of state, all of whom are appointed by the president.

The chancellor is the leader of the government and interacts with parliament. The Austrian Parliament is divided into two houses: the National Council which has 165 members elected to four–year terms, and the Federal Council which has fifty members selected by the legislatures of the states.

Each state has its own form of government with a governor and legislative body. The state is further divided into administrative districts and individual communities.

The Austrian Constitution stresses the rights of minorities by incorporating a portion of the 1919 Treaty of St. Germain, but moves toward a strong centralism of governmental control.

Organization of the Police

Police power rests with the national government in the Ministry of the Interior. Police authority is delegated from the national government, to the state, to the community through distinct and well established bureaucratic lines of procedure and communication.

There are two police systems in Austria: (1) the National Police, which consists of uniform and criminal police (detective branch), and (2) the Gendarmerie. In principle, as well as in practice, the National Police and the Gendarmerie are subordinate to the Ministry of the Interior, with the National Police responsible for security and order in urban communities and the Gendarmerie responsible for security and order in rural areas (see Figure 18).

As an example of municipal policing, Vienna is divided into four police functions: (1) general police duties (performed by uniform police); (2) matters dealing with government security; (3) criminal investigation; and (4) administrative affairs (see Figure 19).

The hierarchy of the Gendarmerie begins with the squad which can be found in the rural community. From the squad originate one– and two– man patrols which carry out the enforcement of laws and general police duties. Squads are then formed into pla-

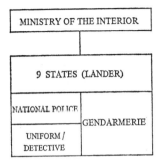

Figure 18. Organization of the Police in Austria, 1969.

toons and other military–style units that carry out the tasks of the Gendarmerie. The force is also responsible for border patrol and rescue work, and it has its own detective units engaged in

Department I
  a. Uniform police

Department II
  a. Security police
  b. Police for aliens
  c. Office for the registration of societies
  d. Office investigating infringements of the press
     (Gerichtliche Presspolizei)

Department III
  a. Criminal investigation (Sicherheitsburo)
  b. Economic crimes (Wirtschaftspolizei)
  c. Records (Fahndungsamt)
    1. Fictitious names
    2. Physical descriptions
    3. Objects and stolen property
    4. Missing persons
    5. Dead bodies (unidentified)
  d. Identification (Erkennungsamt)
    1. Fingerprint files
    2. Crime laboratory
    3. Photography laboratory
  e. Juvenile (female investigators assigned to staff)
  f. Vice (Geschlechtskrankheiten-Madchenhandel)
    1. Prostitution and venereal disease
  g. Criminal register (Strafregisteramt)

Department IV
  a. Motor vehicles
    1. Driver licenses, vehicle registration, planning
      of traffic regulation
  b. Inspection and regulation of licensed business
  c. Lost property
  d. Passport office

Figure 19. Organization of the Vienna Police, 1969.

criminal investigation and prosecution within its geographic jurisdiction.

Selected Readings
Austrian Police Literature

General

Furbock, J. *Sammlung von Reichs– Staats– und Bundesgesetzen sowie sonstigen Vorschriften für den Dienstgebrauch der österreichischen Bundesgendarmerie.* Wien: Selbstverlag, 1960.

Furbock, J. *Gendarmeriegesetze und Dienstinstruktion für die österreichische Bundesgendarmerie.* Wien: Hollinek, 1959.

Gundolf, H. *Gendarmerie im Einsatz.* Innisbruck: Golf-Verlag, 1961.

Kollmann, K. *Uniformierungsvorschrift für die österreichische Bundesgendarmerie.* Wien: Österreichische Staatsduckerei, 1952.

Mayerhofer, C. *Der Kraftfahrzeugdiebstahl und verwandte Delikte.* Wien: Springer Verlag, 1962.

Schmittner, P. *Dienstbuch für die Sicherheitswache.* Wien: Amtsdruckerei der Bundespolizeidirektion, 1953.

Schönemann, D. *Wiener Polizei. Die Physiognomie der Handschrift.*
Experimentelle Untersuchung zur gestaltanalytischen Graphologie. Graz: Diss, 1959.

Springer, K. *Die Österreichische Polizei; Eine theoretische Untersuchung.* Innisbruck: Golf-Verlag, 1960.

Ringel, E. *Neue Untersuchungen zum Selbstmordproblem; unter Berücksichtigung prophylaktischer Gesichtspunkte.* Wien: Hollinek, 1962.

Periodicals and Journals

Die Exekutive. Kameradschaft de Exekutive Osterreichs. Laudongasse 16, Wien VIII.

Illustrierte Rundschau der Gendarmerie. Landstrasser Hauptstrasse 68, Wien III.

Oeffentliche Sicherheit. Bundesministerium für Inneres, direktion für die öffentliche Sicherheit.

II. BELGIUM
Political Traits

Belgium is approximately 12,000 square miles in area and has a population of about ten million persons.

Belgium is a constitutional monarchy, the king being head of state. The position is hereditary and passes from father to son unless challenged by parliament. The king is primarily a symbol of the national government and does not actively generate power or exercise administrative leadership. The premier and his cabinet, appointed by the king, are responsible for executive leadership.

Parliament consists of the Senate, which is made up of 175 members serving four–year terms, and the Chamber of Representatives, which has 212 members who also serve four–year terms.

Belgium consists of nine states (provinces); each has a governor and legislative council. The nine states are divided into 230 counties (cantons).

One of the difficulties in Belgium is the existence of two official languages: Flemish and French. Unlike Switzerland, which fortunately has minimized the tensions that can develop between two unique ethnic groups, the Belgians have a certain division, as Flemish is spoken and written in the north of the country, while in the south French is the official language. Schools, libraries, police, and other public institutions are constantly caught in the conflict of language and culture. The general elections of 1968 brought the conflict into the open through demonstrations and other public disturbances of young and old alike. The government has attempted to decentralize its activities based upon linguistic–ethnic–cultural boundaries. The problem of community relations and public service is complex at best and nonoperative at its worst.

Legal Characteristics

The Belgian king appoints judges for life on the recommendation of the Ministry of Justice. The highest legal authority is the Assize court, one for each state. The country is divided into twenty–six legal districts. Each legal district has its own Criminal Court of First Instance, and is then subdivided into 230 judicial counties (cantons), each of which has its own Justice of the Peace. (See Figure 20 for a description of the judicial system.)

Organization of the Police

There are three police systems in Belgium: (1) the Community Police; (2) Judicial Criminal Police; and (3) the Gendarmerie.

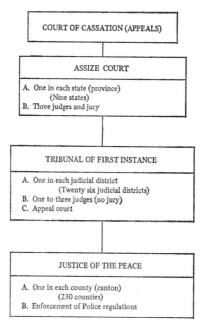

Figure 20. The judicial system of Belgium, 1969.

(See Figure 21 for an organizational structure of the police in Belgium.)

The Community Police are responsible to the mayor in each jurisdiction and respond to the Minister of the Interior for overall direction and coordination.[2] The police perform ordinary police duties including general patrol and traffic. The Community Police conduct preliminary investigations of crimes, but are then required to turn the case over to the Judicial Criminal Police.

The Judicial Criminal Police conduct further investigations and when a defendant is found, prepare the case for court presentation and assist the prosecution for trial.

The Gendarmerie is directly responsible to the Minister of National Defense but also relates to the Minister of Justice, the Judicial Criminal Police, the Minister of the Interior, and the Community Police. In addition to patrol and protection of rural

2. *Rapport du service de la police* (Bruxelles: Imprimerie H. et M. Schaumans, 1968), pp. 1–45.

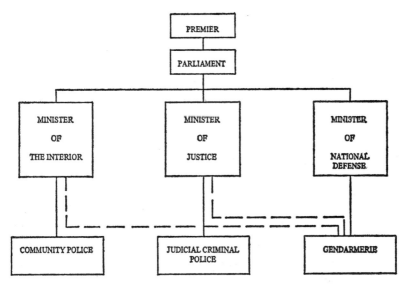

Figure 21. Organization of the Police in Belgium, 1969.

areas, the Gendarmerie protects borders, conducts rescues, and supplies mobile units for crowd control.[3]

Selected Readings

Belgian Police Literature

General

Beauprez, P. *Vaststelling van verkeersongevallen.* Antwerpen: Standaard Boekhandel, 1961.

De Laet, M. *Abrégé de médecine légale criminelle et de criminalistique.* Brussel: De Visscher, 1950.

Louwage, F. & Van der Auwermeulen. *Politiehandboek.* Gent: Editions Edipoli, 1962.

Rommel, J. *Administratief Lexicon.* Brugge: Uitg. Die Keure.

Periodicals and Journals

De Politieofficier. Nationale Federatie der Kommissarissen van politie en adjunct-kommissarissen van politie van België. Kerkeveldstraat, 49, Bruxelles 2.

De Revue van de Rijkswacht. Rijkswacht, Kroonlaan 229, Bruxelles 5.

---

3. *Organisation générale.* (Bruxelles: École Royale de Gendarmerie, 1969), pp. 1–15.

Politieschool in de Huiskamer. Nationaal Syndicaat der Belgische Politie
    Bruxelles.
Revue de la Gendarmerie. 47, rue Fritz Toussaint, Bruxelles 5.

III. FRANCE

Political Traits

There are approximately fifty million people in France, which
is 212,659 square miles in area. Historically, political changes have
occurred with great frequency. It has been estimated that France
"has changed its form of government an average of once every
eighteen years." [4] The French appear to be very individualistic
in political choices as well as in other areas in which decisions
are needed. Because of their individualistic attitude in governmental affairs and the formation of a great diversity of political
parties, there are many cleavages among the French people. Opposition to authority is characteristic when authority is presented
in either direct or in decentralized form. With various political
factions developing conflict and social strife, local governments
seem inadequate in dealing with basic public needs. The system
has been described in the following way:

> The characteristic French form of authority is thus centralized
> authority. Local governments and voluntary associations are weak;
> citizens expect the national government to take major responsibility
> for settling strikes when they occur, helping industries to prosper
> and assuring citizens' welfare. The French prefer authority to be
> centralized and distant, which, in turn, frees them to oppose im-
> mediate authority (and helps to explain why the French have been
> called a race of *rouspéteurs*—grumblers).[5]

France can best be identified as a democratic republic. It has
a president, prime minister, and a parliament. The Fifth Republic
was created in 1958 after the approval of a new constitution. One
of the areas of improvement during the Fifth Republic was the
result of the passage of Assembly Law No. 66–492, which effected
the combining in 1966 of two traditionally autonomous French
police forces: the Préfecture of Police of Paris and the Sûreté
Nationale. Direction of the new centralized police force became

4. Mark Kesselman: *France: The Gaullist Era and After* (New York: Foreign
Policy Association, Inc. April 1969), p. 3.
5. *Ibid.,* pp. 7–8.

the duty of the Secretary General of Police. However, the force remained decentralized geographically.

Legal Characteristics

French law is based upon statutes and decrees. Statute law has greater importance in that

> The statute is supreme as a source of law: the courts must apply it and are not entitled to question the validity or constitutionality of a duly promulgated statute. Moreover, a judge may not refuse to decide a case because of the silence, obscurity or insufficiency of the law.[6]

The structure of the court system moves from the lower courts to the courts of appeal, which deal with civil and less serious criminal cases; to courts of assizes, which hear cases dealing with serious crimes; and, finally, to the court of cassation which is the highest court of France in cases of appeals.[7]

Organization of the Police

There are two police forces in France: (1) the Police Nationale, and (2) the Gendarmerie Nationale. (Refer to Figure 22 for a historical outline of the French police.)

In July 1966, Assembly Law No. 66–492 was passed. It combined the Paris police and the Sûreté Nationale into what is now called the Police Nationale (see Figure 23 for the organization of the Police Nationale).

The Police Nationale has approximately 90,000 personnel, who are responsible to the Minister of the Interior. The Police Nationale is responsible for policing in cities with a population of 10,000 or more. There are two primary departments to the Police Nationale: [8]

---

6. Charles Szladits: *Guide to Foreign Legal Materials: French, German, Swiss* (New York: Oceana Publications, Inc., 1959), p. 5.

7. Refer to Jean Larguier, *Droit Pénal Général et Procédure Pénale* (Paris: Librairie Dalloz, 1968), and Robert Vouin, 2nd ed., *Droit Pénal Spécial* (Paris: Librairie Dalloz, 1968). "Cassation" is the French word for the juridical decision-making regarding arrests and summonses, etc. (the *cour de cassation* is the supreme court).

8. For material prior to amalgamation see P. J. Stead: "The Police of France," *Medico-Legal Journal*, vol. 33 (1965), pp. 3–11; Marcel Le Clère: *Histoire de La Police*, 3rd ed. (Paris: Presses Universitaires de France, 1964); and *La Sûreté Nationale* (Paris: Ministère de l'Intérieur, n.d.) published prior to 1966.

∞∞∞∞∞ POLICE EVENT ∞∞∞∞∞

Date	
615	Clotaire II institutes commissaires–enquêteurs to maintain the peace.
803	Charlemagne's edict on their duties and on those of the watch.
1032	Henri I institutes Prévôt of Paris.
1254	Louis IX institutes royal watch under Chevalier du Guêt.
1306	A commissaire-enquêteur au Châtelet appointed for each "quartier" of Paris.
1524	Francis I appoints enquêteurs-examinateurs in bailliages and prévôtes in the provinces.
1544	Organization of the maréchaussée, military police.
1667	Reorganization of the Paris police by Louis XIV. Installation of Lieutenant-General of Police.
1699	Commissaires of police instituted in principal provincial centers.
1789	Revolution. The last Lieutenant-General, Thiroux de Crosne, hands over the police to Bailly, Mayor of Paris, and provisional police committee.
1790	Decree creates 48 commissaires of police for Paris, elected every two years.
1791	Law creating commissaires of police "wherever necessary."
1799	Fouché appointed Minister of Police.
1800	Establishment of the Préfecture of Police of Paris.
1802	Napoleon abolishes the Ministry of Police.
1804	Napoleon restores the Ministry of Police. Fouché appointed Minister.
1808	Code of Criminal Procedure.
1810	Penal Code. Fouché dismissed.
1815	Fouché appointed Minister of Police (The Hundred Days) by Napoleon. Fouché appointed Minister of Police by Louis XVIII. (He left France in October and died in exile in 1820.)
1811–27	E. F. Vidocq creates the Sûreté branch at the Préfecture of Police.
1829	The sergents de ville police the Paris streets.
1830	Revolution. Louis-Philippe becomes King.
1832	Reorganization of the Sûreté at the Préfecture.
1848	Revolution. Second Republic.
1851	Coup d'état. Napoleon III becomes Emperor. Lyon given a state police.

1854	Central Commissaires instituted in cities with several commissaires of police.
	Paris adopts the London system of beat policing.
1855	State police of railways.
1856	Political police squads instituted.
1870–1	Franco-Prussian War. Third Republic. Corps of "gardiens de la paix" instituted. Sûreté Général founded.
1883	Préfecture's training school for policemen founded.
1883–1914	A. Bertillon at the Préfecture of Police.
1884	Préfects given police power in towns of 40,000 or more population.
1893	Fingerprinting adopted.
1894	Renseignements Généraux branch instituted (Police general intelligence).
1897–99	Direction de la Surveillance du Territoire instituted (Police counter-espionage branch).
1903	Law defining police functions of the Gendarmerie.
1907	Regional detective squads formed by Clémenceau.
1908	Marseilles given state police.
1910	E. Locard starts Forensic Science Laboratory in Lyon.
1923	Interpol begins in Vienna (headquarters in Paris since 1946).
1934	February riots in Paris (Communists and Fascists).
1935	Préfecture's officer training college founded.
1940	Fall of France. Germans occupy Paris. Vichy State set up under Marshal Pétain.
1941	State police given to towns with 10,000 or more inhabitants. Foundation of Sûreté's Police College at St. Cyr–au–Mont–d'Or near Lyon.
1944	German garrison commander surrenders at Préfecture of Police.
1945	Formation of C. R. S. (Republican Security Companies).
1948	Police deprived of the right to strike.
1959	Code of Penal Procedure.
1966	Law of 31st of July integrates personnel of Préfecture of Police and Sûreté Nationale and creates office of Secretary–General of Police at Ministry of the Interior.
1969	Secretary–General becomes Director–General of the National Police.

Figure 22. Historical outline of the French Police. Lecture hand-out developed by Philip John Stead, Dean of General Studies, Police College, Bramshill, England.

1. *The Direction de la Sécurité Publique,* which is known as the S. P., is the general uniform patrol utilized throughout France. The S. P. is further divided into the Corps Urbains, which is re-

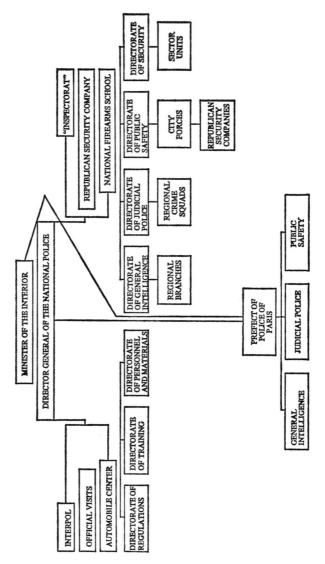

Figure 23. Organization of the Police Nationale, 1970.

sponsible for patrol and traffic duties in municipalities, and the Compagnies Républicaines de Sécurité, which are also known as the C.R.S. The C.R.S. is a paramilitary force of approximately 15,000 policemen. The primary function of this group is the control of public order and security during social unrest. In actual practice, a large part of this section can be brought together for riot control in any geographic area of France. Additional responsibilities include border patrol and search–and–rescue operations.

2. *The Police Judiciaire* is the detective or criminal investigation branch. The Police Judiciaire is responsible to the public prosecutors and magistrates for the investigation of criminal cases. Such things as homicides, robbery, theft, etc., are handled by these detectives, as are initial investigations, follow–up investigations based on citizen complaints or patrol officers' reports, arrests, and presentation of evidence to the courts.

There are also: (1) the Directeur des Renseignements Généraux et des Jeux, who deals with criminal activities such as vice, gambling, and so on; and (2) the Directeur de la Surveillance du Territoire, who deals with counter–espionage, subversion, and political crimes.

In addition to the Police Nationale,[9] there is a second body of police in France called **the Gendarmerie Nationale.** There are approximately 60,000 personnel in the Gendarmerie, a military force whose main responsibility is policing. It is under the direction of the Minister for the Armies and shares the dual task of policing the military as well as the civilian population. Rural areas, with towns of less than 10,000 in population, are policed by the Gendarmerie. Some of its personnel, however, are assigned to the judicial police and take part in criminal investigations in communities with a population of under 10,000 and also aid in prosecutions.

There are several special units in the Gendarmerie Nationale which should be further identified: (1) the Garde Républicaine of Paris which participates in general police work in the capital city, as well serving as honor guard for ceremonial occasions; (2) the Gendarmerie Maritime which specializes in policing harbors, military arsenals, and military components of the Navy and Air Force; and (3) the Gendarmerie de l'Air—la Gendarmerie des Transports Aériens, which is responsible for the public and military security of aerial transport.

---

9. See the following for a description on police recognition: "Organization et perspectives de la Police nationale," *Revue de la défénse nationale,* févr. 1968.

French police personnel, the Police Nationale, or Gendarmerie Nationale, are considered on duty at all times. The police are not allowed to hold political office. Policemen are permitted to form trade unions, but are forbidden by a 1948 law to strike actively. However, on occasion the police have used such tactics as slowing down work productivity or calling in sick to express discontent over job inequities. The police in Paris during March 1971 used these tactics, in addition to debating with citizens in the streets in an effort to present the police cause. In France there are approximately three policemen per one thousand inhabitants.

There are no policewomen in France. There is, however, a special unit called "Assistantes de Police" in the Police Nationale, which is staffed in part by women. They are concerned with the prevention of juvenile delinquency. They counsel young people and families, and act as a referral source to public and private agencies.

Recruitment into the Police Nationale is based upon lateral entry as well as promotion from within the organization. The level of education and the aspirations of the individual often tend to separate the uniform and detective branches. More educated persons seek positions in detective and administrative areas within the police, while generally (though not always) the less educated take positions in the uniform branches.

POLICE NATIONALE: The Police Nationale can be divided into five sub–organizations. Each is a separate structure and has individual qualifications and requirements for acceptance and promotion. (See Figure 24 for a comparison of career employment areas in the Police Nationale.)

The largest group of police personnel in the Police Nationale is the uniform branch Corps des Gradés et Gardiens de La Paix. This group receives an initial six–months period of training: four months consisting of police law, patrol procedures, traffic investigation, weapons training, physical fitness and self–defense; and the remaining two months dealing with practical application in field situations.

Police personnel in various career structures receive different training programs: the "Corps des Officiers de Police Adjoints" receives approximately four months of training in criminal law,

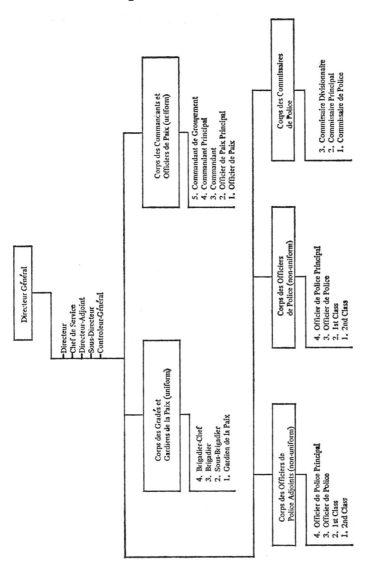

Figure 24. Organization of the Police Nationale by career area and classification of rank within each career structure, 1970.

crime investigation, criminology, and police administration; the "Officiers de Paix" receive a five–month course dealing with government, sociology, psychology, criminology, police organization and management, investigation, criminalistics, and physical education and self–defense; the "Corps des Commissaires de Police" receives the same training as the Officiers de Paix but in greater depth.

Lateral entry into the Police Nationale depends on successfully passing written and oral examinations in competition with personnel from within the ranks. Applicants from the outside seeking higher posts in the Police Nationale must hold university degrees or the equivalent.

GENDARMERIE NATIONALE: The Gendarmerie Nationale can be divided into enlisted and officer personnel. Enlisted personnel receive a basic six–month course of instruction in police and military subjects. A course for officers lasts approximately ten months and deals with specifics of law, organization, general education, military subjects, and physical education.

An automatic pistol (7.65 mm) is carried by police personnel in addition to a truncheon. However, larger caliber weapons can be supplied to personnel if there is need.

Selected Readings
French Police Literature

General

Berenyi, Ivan: "The Changing Profile of the French Police," *Police Review,* October 24, 1969, pp. 1-2.

Décret No. 67–196 du 14 mars 1967 portant réorganisation du Ministère de l'Intérieur.

"France: Crime Statistics," *International Criminal Police Review,* May 1965, No. 188, pp. 126–134.

Hawkins, H. J. "The C.R.S.," *Police Journal,* Vol. XLIV, no. 2, April-June 1971, pp. 129–132.

Hawkins, H. J. "The Police Career in France," *Police Journal,* May 1970, pp. 214-221.

Le Clère, Marcel: *Histoire de la Police,* 3 ed. Paris: Presses Universitaires de France, 1964.

Loi No. 66–492 du 9 juillet 1961 portant organisation de la Police Nationale.

"Organisation et perspectives de la Police nationale," *Revue de la défense nationale,* fevr. 1968.

Stead, Philip John: *The Police of Paris.* London: Staples Press Limited, 1957.

Stead, Philip John: "The Police of France," *Medico-Legal Journal*, Vol. 33 (1965), pp. 3–11.

"The 1968 Reform of the French Police," *International Criminal Police Review*, January 1969, no. 224, pp. 2–7.

Periodicals and Journals

Chroniques internationales de police. Fédération Internationale des Fonctionaires Supérieurs de Police, Paris.

Gendarmerie Nationale. Direction de la Gendarmerie et de la Justice Militaire, Paris 7e.

Police Revue. Rédaction-Administration, 132 rue de Rivoli, Paris.

Revue d'Études et d' Information de la Gendarmerie Nationale. Gendarmerie Nationale, Paris.

Revue internationale de police criminelle. I.C.P.O. Interpol, 26 rue Armengaud, 92 Saint–Cloud.

Revue Moderne de la Police. Fédération Internationale des Fonctionnaires: Supérieurs de Police, Paris.

Revue Sûreté Nationale. 11 rue Cambacérès, Paris 8e.

IV. GERMANY (WEST)

Political Traits

West Germany has a population of approximately sixty million inhabitants with an estimated density of 650 persons per square mile. Land area is approximately 96,000 square miles.

The national government is a constitutional federal republic which came into being in 1949. The federal republic is made up of ten states plus West Berlin. Each state (länd) has its own regional administration and legislative body.

There is a president who is the honorary head of state, the chancellor who is the head of the government, and a parliament which is divided into two houses.

Parliament selects a member of the strongest political party to be chancellor and, with electors from the various state legislative bodies, selects a president. The presidency is titular in function, and the major thrust for direction comes from the chancellor and parliament.

Each state has its own state government and is headed by a minister, a president, and his cabinet.

The German national character has been identified in the past as law–abiding and rule–oriented.[10] This traditional attitude is changing as the following statement suggests:

> The 1960's saw the emergence of more relaxed cultural and authority patterns. These ranged all the way from a greater willingness to walk on the grass to eased authority patterns in the home, school and place of work. Of particular importance . . . was the willingness to question the established way of conducting politics and to challenge traditional notions of law and order.[11]

The responsibility of the police in Germany has historically been almost total involvement with the community. During the early 1900's the police were engaged in routine police work as well as in directing the unemployment insurance benefit program, regulating fire laws, and licensing and inspecting certain businesses. A police official in the 1920's declared:

> Generally speaking the interest of the state and its citizens does not allow for any curtailment in the police's range of activities. On the contrary, this area must be constantly enlarged in accordance with the changing conditions of life.[12]

Legal Characteristics

German law is based upon statutes and decrees. The present form of criminal law is founded upon the Code of Criminal Procedure of February, 1871. This code has been amended several times but continues to be the main source for criminal procedure in Germany.

The administration of justice is divided between federal courts and state courts. The federal courts deal with federal law, whereas state courts deal with both federal and state law. The states (länder) are individually responsible for the administration of justice in their respective geographic territory. The uniformity of the state courts is maintained by the Law of the Constitution of the Courts.

The legal basis of the German criminal law is the Penal Code

---

10. This characteristic has been documented by writers of law enforcement for many years. As an example refer to Raymond B. Fosdick: *European Police Systems* (New York: Century Co., 1915) and his comments on the German police.

11. Richard L. Merritt and Anna J. Merritt: *West Germany Enters the Seventies* (New York: Foreign Policy Association, Inc., April 1971), p. 6.

12. Menzel, "Reformmoglichkeiten bei der Polizei," *Die Polizei*, 25 Hng., Nr. 2, Jan. 20, 1928, pp. 31–32, as cited in Hsi-Huey Liang: *The Berlin Police Force in the Weimar Republic* (Berkeley: University of California Press, 1970), p. 9.

of 1871 (see Appendix C). This basic instrument has been amended over the years, and at the present time (1973) is receiving major revision. Up to now the code divided criminal acts into felonies, offenses, and misdemeanors. A criminal act which is punishable with one year or more of imprisonment, is classified as a felony, i. e. murder, robbery, perjury. An act, which is punishable with six weeks or less in prison or by a monetary fine up to a specific amount, is identified as a misdemeanor. All other acts involving the possibility of imprisonment or a fine are identified as offenses, i.e. fraud, larceny, manslaughter.

In criminal cases the normal progress is from the lower courts to the upper courts, that is, county court to land court, upward to higher land court, and finally to the federal court of justice (see Figure 25 for a comparison of court characteristics).

Organization of the Police

There are approximately 120,000 police in West Germany. There are 100,000 state police, 18,000 municipal police, and about 2,000 railway police. In addition, there are criminal police, emergency police, and water police. The German police have adopted the motto "The policeman—your friend and helper," [13] which is in accordance with the basic German police philosophy of total involvement in the community.

After the collapse of the Third Reich in 1945 the German police were reorganized into individual state police forces. Each of the ten state police and West Berlin police respond to laws pertaining to regional matters and administration. The individual state has autonomy in directing its police.

The police can be divided into the following areas: state police, municipal police, criminal police, emergency police, water police, and railway police.

The state police are responsible for general patrol and traffic duties in the rural areas and smaller towns. Municipal police are of course found in the larger cities. The criminal police are situated locally as well as regionally, and are organized to function

13. Reference is made to the article by George Berkley: "The European Police: Challenge and Change," *Public Administration Review*, vol. 28, no. 5, September–October 1968, pp. 424–430.

	CRIMINALITY OF MINOR OR INTERMEDIATE SERIOUSNESS	SERIOUS CRIMINALITY	CASES CONCERNING PROTECTION OF THE STATE (High treason and betrayal of country)
FEDERAL COURT OF JUSTICE	Criminal Senate, 5 Judges	Criminal Senate, 5 Judges	Criminal Senate, 5 Judges
HIGHER LAND COURT	Criminal Senate, 3 Judges		Criminal Senate, 5 Judges
LAND COURT	Small Criminal Chamber, 1 Judge, 2 Jurors / Grand Criminal Chamber, 3 Judges, 2 Jurors / Juvenile Chamber, 3 Judges, 2 Juvenile Jurors	Grand Criminal Chamber, 3 Judges, 2 Jurors / Assize Court, 3 Judges, 6 Members of the Jury / Juvenile Chamber, 3 Judges, 2 Juvenile Jurors	
COUNTY COURT	Judge (Sitting Alone) / Jury-Court, 1 Judge, 2 Jurors or Enlarged Jury-Court 2 Judges, 2 Jurors / Judge for Juveniles or Juvenile Jury-Court 1 Judge, 2 Juvenile Jurors		

Figure 25. Comparison of German Court characteristics. Movement of appeal is from lower court to next higher court. Adapted from Wolfgang Heyde: *The Administration of Justice in the Federal Republic of Germany* (Berlin: Press and Information Office of the Federal Government, 1971), pp. 67-75.

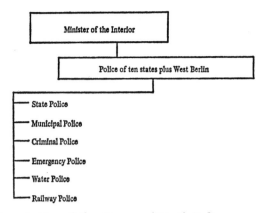

Figure 26. Organization of the German (West) Police.

like the British detectives. The emergency police are a special force that deal with riots, disasters, and any other problems that can be identified as emergencies. The water police and railway police have jurisdiction in their respective areas. (See Figure 26 for a description of the various organizations.)

There are training schools in each state. After the applicant has met the basic entrance requirements—sufficient education, high personal character, good health, and other prerequisites, he attends a basic police course at the local state training school, which may last one year. The recruit must have a combination of training and approximately three years practical experience before he is recognized as a policeman. Around 25 per cent of his basic police training time is devoted to studying history, psychology, and government.

In addition to the individual state training schools, there is a Police Institute at Hiltrup for senior command officers. The Institute is residential and the courses last from six to nine months. The Institute is supported by the Federal Republic of Germany, the ten separate states, and West Berlin.

A board of governors is formed from representatives of all the states and the federal government. Supervision of the Institute comes from the Ministry of the Interior.

The main function of the Institute is to provide standardized training for police officers who are qualified for promotion to senior positions within the police. The course lasts about six months.

There is also a course dealing with training of police instructors in the Institute's department of teacher training. Some of the courses, especially those run by the Institute's department of teacher training, are also attended by officials of different branches of the German civil administration. The Institute's staff consists of full–time teachers from all of Germany's state police organizations.

The Institute is also involved in the evaluation of police research. Such areas as tactics, criminalistics, criminology, traffic, civics, sociology, and psychology have received some form of inquiry and evaluation by the staff.

Police personnel from other countries have developed exchange programs with the Institute. A comparative and international approach to the study of police work is accepted as a primary learning process at the Institute.

Since 1966 the German police have been prohibited from violating the civil rights of persons to be arrested. The policeman must inform the person of his right to have counsel during interrogation and of all other matters concerning his rights as an individual. The arrestee cannot be the object of deception, coercion, or physical abuse.

All German uniform policemen normally carry a pistol and truncheon while on patrol.

Selected Readings
German Police Literature

General

Bartsch, G. *Der kriminalpolizeiliche Dienst.* Hamburg: Verl. Deutsche Polizei, 1960.

Bochalli, A. *Besonderes Verwaltungsrecht.* Köln: Carl Heymanns Verlag, 1959.

Bochalli, A. *Bundesbeamtengesetz.* München: C H Beck'sche Verlagsbuchhandlung, 1965.

Dirks, Heinz: *Psychologie, eine moderne Seelenkunde.* Bielefeld: Verlag Bertelsmann, 1962.

Georges, B. *Polizei und staátsbürger.* Köln: C. Heymanns Verlag, 1956.

Gintzel, K. *Die polizeilichen Eingriffsbefugnisse.* Lübeck: Schmidt-Römhild, 1967.

Hausen, F. and L. Schweers: *Die Zwangsmittel der Polizei.* Köln: Heymanns Verlag, 1967.

Heinrich, W. *Meister der Kriminalistik.* Berlin: Universitäts–Verlag, 1955.

Knoche, H. *Schriftverkehr im Dienst der Polizeibeamten.* Lübeck: Verlag Schmidt–Römhild, 1960.

Meitz, W. *Allgemeines Polizeirecht in Theorie und polizeilicher Praxis.* Lübeck: Schmidt-Römhild, 1960.

Rehm, M. *Das Planspiel als Bildungsmittel.* Heidelberg: Verlag Quelle und Meyer, 1964.

Scheffler, H. *Kleiner Strafrechtslehrgang.* Lübeck: Verlag Schmidt-Römhild, 1965.

Scheffler, H. *Strafprozessrecht fur Polizeibeamte.* Hamburg: Verlag Deutsche Polizei, 1965.

Schweers, L. *Polizeidienstkunde.* Lübeck: Schmidt-Römhild, 1968.

Wieking, F. and G. Gipkens: *Die Entwicklung der weiblichen Kriminalpolizei in Deutchland.* Lübeck: Schmidt-Römhild, 1958.

Periodicals and Journals

Archiv für Kriminologie. Schmidt-Römhild Verlag, Lübeck.

Deutsche Polizei. Verlag Deutsche Polizei, Hamburg.

Die Neue Polizei. Verlag Rich. Pflaum, München.

Die Polizei. C. Heymanns Verlag, Berlin–Köln.

Kriminalistik. Verlag fur kriminalistische Fachliteratur, Hamburg.

Polizei Technik Verkehr. Deutscher Verkehrsschutz–Verlag, Juliusstr. 2, Wiesbaden.

Polizei–Spiegel. Steintor–Verlag, Hamburg.

V. ITALY

Political Traits

The population of Italy consists of approximately fifty million persons living in a land area of 116,000 square miles.

The present national government of Italy was established on January 1, 1948. At that time a parliamentary republic was created, headed by a president, a premier, and a cabinet, with the parliament divided into two houses consisting of the chamber of deputies and the senate. For administrative purposes Italy is divided into twenty regions and ninety-two provinces; a prefect is the chief administrator of each province and is appointed by the Minister of the Interior.

The president is selected by both houses of parliament for a seven–year term. One condition of being president is that the electee must be at least fifty years of age. The president appoints the premier who must be a member of the chamber of deputies. The president must obtain approval from parliament for his choice. The president has the power to dissolve parliament and request new elections to be held. The premier has no fixed tenure of office and can be removed at any time by parliament.

At the present time there are nineteen Ministries. Three of these have direct responsibility for criminal justice in Italy: (1) the Ministry of the Interior, (2) the Ministry of Justice, and (3) the Ministry of Defense.

The Ministry of the Interior was reorganized in October 1961, under Presidential Decree No. 225. There are nine administrative departments. The Department of Public Security is directly responsible for the maintenance of law and order and public security. To aid in the task of public security, an Office of Prefectures has been established in all the provinces except Trento and Bolzano. Each Prefecture is headed by a prefect whose responsibilities range from the maintainance of public security with various police organizations to the supervision of the general trends of public administration in the province. The Public Administrator is part of the provincial office of the Public Security Branch and is also under the supervision of the Ministry of the Interior.

The Ministry of Justice was first formed in December 1850, by Royal Decree No. 1122. There are four Departments of General Affairs. The administrators of these departments are magistrates of the Supreme Court. The departments are further divided into offices, generally headed by magistrates of the Courts of Appeal.

In addition to the Departments of General Affairs, there are the following: a Department for Civil Affairs and the Professions which is responsible for matters concerning those professions related to the administration of justice; the Department for Penal Affairs, Pardons, and Records which is responsible for the administration of penal law and criminal records; and the Department for Prisons and Penal Institutions.

The Ministry of Defense was reorganized under a decree of February 1947, that merged the Departments of War, Navy, and Air Force. The centralized military and technical organization includes the Secretary General for Defense and specialized offices: legal and legislative, budget and financial affairs, methodological structure, mechanization and statistics, military training, and inspection of administration.

Legal Characteristics

The majority of judges in Italy are appointed on the basis of open civil service examinations. All courts are under the direction of the Minister of Justice and the Superior Council of the Judiciary.[14]

Offenses are classified into crimes and misdemeanors on the basis of their seriousness as anti-social behavior.

The court system consists of the following courts: Praetor, Assizes and Tribunals, Appeals Courts, and the Supreme Court.

The Praetor Court consists of a single judge with no jury who hears criminal cases which can receive a maximum penalty of three years imprisonment and/or a fine.

The Tribunal Court has three judges and hears cases of a more serious nature. However, the Assize Court hears the more serious criminal cases such as homicide, manslaughter, robbery, theft, and so forth, and has two judges with six lay judges.

Courts of Appeal are separated to hear appeals from Assizes and Tribunals.

The Supreme Court is the final area for appeal, but here only legal aspects are re–examined. (See Figure 27 for a comparison of the criminal court system in Italy.)

In addition to the various police organizations and levels of courts, there is also a Public Prosecutor. The public prosecutor is specifically concerned with safeguarding public interest in civil as well as criminal action. In criminal cases the prosecutor intervenes when the offense or crime is committed against an institution or principle representing public affairs. In essence, the public

---

14. Refer to Mauro Cappelletti et al: *The Italian Legal System: An Introduction,* (Stanford: Stanford University Press, 1967), pp. 79–84.

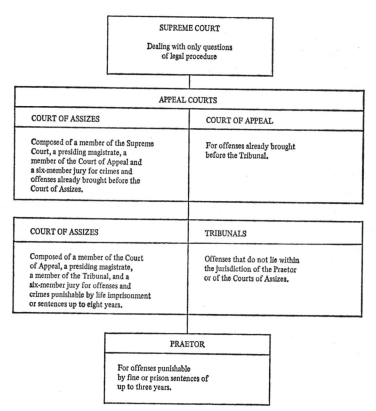

Figure 27. Comparison of the criminal court system of Italy, 1969. Adapted from Presidency of the Council of Ministers, *Constitutional Administration in Italy* (Rome: Information and Copyright Service, 1970), p. 42.

prosecutor is responsible for initiating criminal procedure where matters of public interest are concerned.[15]

The Italian penal system gives discretionary power to the police in the area of arrest when the maximum punishment is three years imprisonment or less for an offense. Arrest is compulsory when the offense is punishable by more than three years in prison. Moreover it is compulsory for those who have been declared habitual or professional criminals. An arrest is also compulsory when a complaint is made by the plaintiff.

15. Presidency of the Council of Ministers, *Constitutional Administration in Italy.* (Rome: Information and Copyright Service, 1970) pp. 42–43.

Organization of the Police

There are four police systems functioning in Italy. Three are of a national character: the military police (Carabinieri); the public security police (Guardie di Pubblica Sicurezza); and the treasury police (Guardie di Finanza). The fourth police system is the local community police (Vigili Urbani).

These police systems are predominantly independent. In an attempt to coordinate their activities at the detective investigative level, a coordinating organization was established in March 1967 called the National Center for the Coordination of Criminal Police Operations (Criminalpol).

Criminalpol coordinates the activities of the four principal police systems in Italy. In particular, it gathers information likely to lead to the prevention and repression of the more serious forms of crime (homicide, robbery, the unlawful sale of arms and drugs, etc.); serves as liaison between all police units and the various special departments of the Public Security Police; makes improvements in the standard of criminal police services through the development of the information network which maintains a constant and extensive exchange of information and technical experience; organizes emergency plans; maintains preventive services in general; and analyzes and studies the various requirements which may arise in connection with criminal police operations and problems related to delinquency.

To enable it to carry out its extensive and complex tasks, the National Criminalpol Center is divided into eight sections: general affairs and personnel; crimes against property and statistics; stolen vehicles; crimes against the person and preventive measures; Interpol; technical investigation and documentation; identification; and regional supervision. In addition, there is a military police liaison office and a crime prevention office. (See Figure 28 for a description of the Criminalpol organization. Reference should also be made here to Figure 29, which describes the relationship of the four police systems in Italy.) Each police agency operates independently although the National Criminalpol Center is attempting to develop liaison and coordination of field operations.

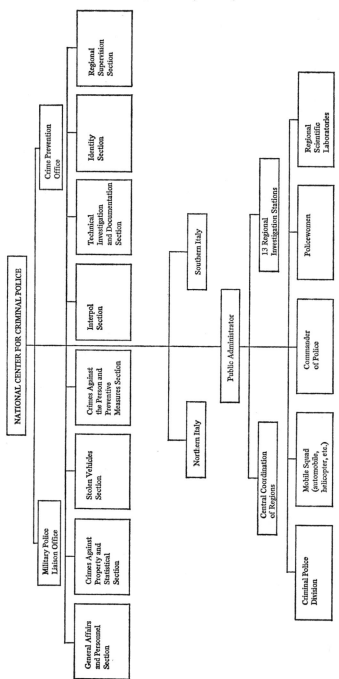

Figure 28. Organization of Criminalpol for Italy, 1969.

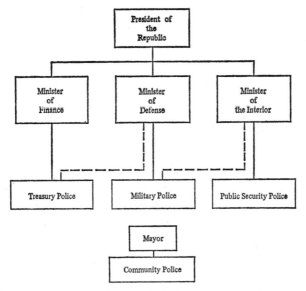

Figure 29. Organizational relation of the four Italian Police Forces, 1969.

MILITARY POLICE (CARABINIERI). There are approximately 80,000 military police in Italy who have the dual role of policing the military forces and policing the civilian population. The military police are responsible to the Minister of Defense for technical and military support, while it is also responsible to the Minister of the Interior for all police duties involved in the protection of life and property.[16] As this would indicate, the role of the military police in Italy is very flexible. Deployment of these personnel depends on the density of population and the availability of other operational police systems. Therefore, the military police can be found in all parts of Italy, rural as well as urban.

Military police follow traditional military concepts of training, uniforms, ranks, identification, recruitment into enlisted and officer groups, and total general army regimentation.

PUBLIC SECURITY POLICE (GUARDIE DI PUBBLICA SICUREZZA). Whereas the military police is a formal component of the Italian Army, the public security police is similar in organization to a

---

16. Information obtained during a visit with personnel of the Comando Generale Dell'Arma, Carabinieri, in Rome, 1969.

national guard force which is responsible to the Minister of the Interior for public security. Like the military police, the public security police serve with the Army in times of emergency.[17]

There are approximately 80,000 men in the public security police. They are divided into three major functions: regional police units dispersed within geographic boundaries throughout Italy; mobile police responsible for crowd control and riot disturbances; and the special police responsible for national traffic control, search, and rescue.

Public security includes the wide spectrum of apprehension, suppression, prevention of acts, and surveillance of persons that can be identified as criminal. In actual practice there appears to be an overlap of responsibilities and field operations between the public security police and the military police in achieving protection of life and property.

TREASURY POLICE (GUARDIE DI FINANZA). The treasury police are responsible for combating smuggling, tax evasion, illegal entry into the country, and counterfeiting. The treasury police is under the control of the Ministry of Finance; however, during times of extreme emergency, this function may become the responsibility of the Minister of Defense. The present structure and organization of the treasury police were established by Article I of Organization Law 189 (April, 1959), which outlines its duties as follows: to prevent and apprehend financial evaders and violators; to carry out investigations; to review political–economic interests; to act as maritime police; to contribute to political–military defense of the frontiers; to convert to military operations in case of war; and to contribute in general to keeping order and public safety.[18]

COMMUNITY POLICE (VIGILI URBANI). The community police are responsible to the local communities under the direction of each mayor. Their function is dual: traffic control and the inspection of certain business operations, (i. e., taxis, markets), for public health standards. It should be remembered that local autonomy is held in high esteem by the resident population, especially where

---

17. *Le Scuole di Polizia in Italia* (Roma: Ministero dell'Interno, Direzione Generale della Pubblica Sicurezza, 1969).
18. *Rivista della Guardia di Finanza*, November–December (No. 6), 1970, p. 28.

the individual (community) police systems are concerned. Although qualifications for selection into the community police vary from city to city, traffic and inspection remain the major function in most of them.

With the development of the National Center for Criminal Police (Criminalpol), an attempt is being made to coordinate the four police systems of Italy. However, consolidation of policies and procedures is difficult to achieve and may prove unpopular with the general public in that country.

Selected Readings
Italian Police Literature

General

Barbaria, A. *Compendio di diritto di Polizia*. Roma: La Navicella, 1960.

Calamante, M. *Manuale dell'agente stradale*. Roma: Guasta, 1952.

DeRossi, A. *Vigili Urbani di Roma*. Roma: Abruzzini, 1954.

DiGirolamo, R. *La Guardia di Pubblica Sicurezza*. Milano: Mottola, 1958.

Ministero Dell'Interno. *La Pubblica Sicurezza nel 1956*. Roma: Ministero dell'Interno, 1957.

Spadaccini, R. *Polizia Giudiziaria e Vigili Urbani*. Bolzano: Presel, 1958.

Virga, P. *La potestà di polizia*. Milano: Hoepli, 1954.

Periodicals and Journals

Bollettino della Scuola di Polizia e Servizi di Segnalazione. Ministerio degli Interni, Roma.

Polizia Moderna. Roma.

Revista Mensile dell'Arma dei Carabinieri. Roma.

Rivista Mensile della Guardia di Finanza. Roma.

Statistica Degli Incidenti Stradali. Automobile Club d'Italia e dell'Istituto Centrale di Statistica, Roma.

VI. THE NETHERLANDS

Political Traits

There are approximately thirteen million persons in the Netherlands with a land area of approximately 14,000 square miles.

The government is a constitutional monarchy. The head of state, from the royal house, appoints the prime minister. The prime minister and his cabinet originate most legislation and must have continued support from the parliament. The head of state also appoints the leaders of both houses of parliament, state governors, and mayors of municipalities.

Parliament is divided into two houses: the first chamber has 75 legislators selected by the provinces, and the second chamber consists of 150 members selected by popular election. Each house can accept or reject possible laws. The second chamber is the primary initiator of bills which may become laws with the approval of both houses.

The Minister of Justice's position in the cabinet is the one responsible for public safety in the Netherlands, through interaction with the attorneys general, the police, and the courts.

Legal Characteristics

Judges in the Netherlands are appointed by the head of state for life. The penal code and criminal procedure code identify crimes according to the seriousness of the offense and assign the responsibility for enforcing criminal laws to the police.

There are three police systems in the Netherlands: (1) the national police (Rijkspolitie), (2) individual municipal police forces (Gemeentepolitie), and (3) the military police (Koninklyka Maréchaussee).

Law enforcement in the Netherlands is regulated by the Police Act of 1957. The act assigns responsibility for the national police to the Minister of Justice, and responsibility for the municipal police to the individual city mayor and the Minister of the Interior.

NATIONAL POLICE. In the Netherlands there are approximately 6,000 national policemen, with the country divided into twenty-three police areas. These, in turn, are further divided into smaller geographic units for the deployment of national police personnel. Generally, the national police responsibility is assigned to the rural communities. Special components of the police are responsible for river patrol, highway patrol, and aviation.

The national police can assist local municipal police when called upon to do so. In times of national emergency or need for crowd control, the national police can utilize its personnel and lines of communication in aiding individual municipalities.

At the national level there are a number of special units in the

Ministry of Justice doing investigative work in the areas of criminalistics, narcotics, international crimes, automobile theft, and other serious crimes.

MUNICIPAL POLICE. The municipal police are located in approximately 122 urban municipalities. The combined strength of municipal police forces adds up to approximately 14,500 men. In each locality the police department is controlled by the mayor (as recognized by the Minister of the Interior) and by the chief of police. (See Figure 30 for an organization chart showing an outline of the Amsterdan municipal police force.)

A more detailed summary [19] follows:

ORGANIZATION OF THE AMSTERDAM POLICE FORCE
I. DEPARTMENT OF THE CHIEF COMMISSIONER
   a. Personnel department
      Treatment of all personnel affairs, such as applications, appointments, dismissals, illnesses, holidays, facilities, punishable behavior of police officers, etc.
      Distribution of incoming correspondence
      Treatment of all affairs regarding the police trade unions
      Police school training of constables and sergeants, refresher courses for the lower ranks, and courses for the police diploma
   b. Secretariat
      Handling of general affairs; juridical advice and correspondence; monthly and annual reports; rewards to policemen; treatment of compensation of damages caused by policemen
      Supervision of central police archives, central typing room and police canteen
      Maintenance of police buildings
      Crime prevention office (telling public how to prevent crimes)
   c. License branch
      Issuance of licenses for liquor, fishing, hunting, weapons, collections, meetings, music, etc.
   d. Financial department
      Financial management, such as administration of wages, purchasing uniforms and supplies
   e. Physical training

19. From an official publication of the Amsterdam police and a personal interview with Dutch police administrators, 1969.

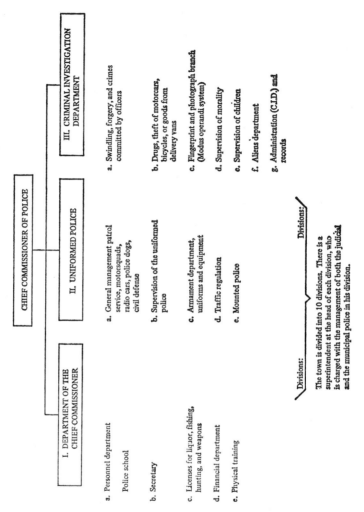

Figure 30. Organizational Chart of the Amsterdam Municipal Police (From an official publication of the Amsterdam police and a personal interview with Dutch police administrators, 1969).

II. UNIFORMED POLICE
Staff Headquarters

a. Organization and management of the uniformed police force; squad patrols, radiocar patrols; crowd control and escort duties on ceremonial occasions
Supervision of police radio, police telex–writers, and police

telephones (The foot and bicycle patrols are directed from the police stations in the divisions.)

Patrol with dogs in the rural districts of Amsterdam

Civil defense

b. Personnel control
c. Armament department

Target practice for the whole police force

Projection of film

d. Traffic police. (The traffic police is centralized at headquarters, regulated by pointsmen, and automatically controlled by motorsquads. The entire force sometimes aids in traffic control.)

Supervision of taxi–cabs, motorcars, motorcycles, carriages, etc.

Responsibility for parking problems and roadbuilding problems

Additional responsibility for police–cars and the repair shop at headquarters

e. Mounted police and horse patrol

Crowd-control duties

Escort duties on ceremonial occasions

III. CRIMINAL INVESTIGATION DEPARTMENT

In principle the C.I.D. in Amsterdam is decentralized so that when a murder is committed in Division number 3, the superintendent of Division 3 is charged with the investigation. However, there are some crimes which can be better handled by a special squad. These crimes are investigated by C.I.D. men from headquarters, irrespective of the division where the crime has been committed. Therefore, we find the following special branches of the C.I.D. at headquarters:

a. Swindling, forgery (banknotes, pictures) and investigation of crimes committed by officers
b. Drugs, theft of motorcars and bicycles, and theft of goods from delivery vans

Stashing ("fencing") of stolen goods

Fingerprint and photograph branch; laboratory; and *modus operandi* system, which lends assistance to the whole force

c. Supervision of morality (exhibitionism, violation, prostitution, abortion)
d. Supervision of children

Investigation of crimes committed by children under the age of 18, unless one of the above mentioned branches is charged with the investigation of that crime

(Crimes in connection with traffic accidents are treated

by the C.I.D. of the division in which the accident took
place.)

e. Aliens branch

f. Criminal records; administration; inquiries to state and local
authorities concerning petitions of mercy; birthday honors;
passports; certificates of good character; issue of lists of
warranted goods; hotel control; and "lost and found"

IV. DIVISIONS

For the purpose of police surveillance Amsterdam is divided
into 10 divisions. There is a superintendent at the head of each
division who is charged with the management of both the judicial and the uniformed municipal police. The administration
of the business in connection with the responsibilities of the
division is carried on at the police station in each division.

Besides these police stations, auxiliary police stations have
been established where necessary in suitable places all over the
city. They are manned by one or more sergeants and constables.

The above mentioned division heads are assisted by two inspectors; one for the municipal police service and one for the
judicial police service.

The rest of the staff at the division police station consists of
inspectors and sergeants, watch commanders, detectives, constables, and one or two administrative officers.

The inspectors, sergeants, and watch commanders are the
immediate supervisors of the constables on duty in the streets.
They are responsible for the discipline in their offices and for
carrying out duties in an authorized manner.

In addition to these patrols, there are horse, motor, and radio
car patrols which are directed from headquarters by the emergency central.

Training for the administrative ranks of the national police
and the municipal police is conducted at the National Police
Training Institute. Formal training covers a period of three years
and deals with law, organization, management, and police procedures.

Initial police training for recruits into both police systems is
one year at a regional training school.

MILITARY POLICE. The military police, under the direction of the
Minister of Defense, number approximately three thousand. They
participate in civilian police functions when requested to do so
by the national police or municipal police. Their primary respon-

sibilities are border control, investigating crimes in the military, and the personal physical protection of the royal family.

SELECTED READINGS

Police Literature of the Netherlands

General

Besluit van 24 december 1957 (Ambtenarenreglement voor de gemeente-politie).

Besluit van 24 december 1957 voor het korps Rijkspolite.

Carp, E. A. et al. *Gerechtlijke psychiatric.* Amsterdam: Scheltema and Holkema, 1956.

Froentjes, W. *Criminalistick als wetenschap.* Leiden: A. W. Sijthoff's, 1953.

Kallenborn, J. W. *Strijd tegen internationale misdadigers. Een historisch document.* Amsterdam: Keesing, 1953.

Kloosterman, S. *De Politiewet. Tekst en commentaar.* Alphen aan den Rijn: Nederlandse politie-organisatie, 1958.

Politiewet van d juli 1957.

Periodicals and Journals

Algemeen. Politieblad van het Koninkrijk der Nederlanden, 's-Gravenhage.

Excerpta Criminologica. 119–123 Herengracht, Amsterdam.

Politiealmanak. Schaafsma & Brouwer, Dokkum, Postbox 10.

Tijdschrift voor de Politie. A. W. Sijthoff's Uitg. Mij. te Leiden.

VII. NORWAY

Political Traits

With a population of nearly 3,800,000 persons and a land area of approximately 125,000 square miles, Norway is a sparsely inhabited country.

The national government is a constitutional monarchy with a king, prime minister, a cabinet, and a parliament.

There are fourteen cabinet members, one of whom is responsible to the Ministry of Justice and Police. A member of parliament cannot hold a cabinet position since it is a separate function.

Members of parliament are elected to four–year terms and represent Norway's twenty counties. Parliament consists of one house, but its members are divided into two groups for discussion and voting purposes. There are thirty–eight members of parliament in one group and 112 members in the other group. A bill must be approved by the lower group and then by the upper group. If there is a disagreement, the entire membership of parliament may be polled and, if two–thirds agree, a bill will be passed into law.

The constitution stresses the freedom, independence, and indivisibility of the nation. The attitude of freedom is held within a framework of law and justice which can be found in the early development of the country. It has been stated that "The land shall be built on law and not by lawlessness laid waste. And he who will not grant justice to others shall not himself enjoy the benefit of law." [20]

There appears to be a high degree of political and social stability within the Norwegian cultural system. A strong Nordic heritage prevails that expresses itself in national pride and an aura of independence.

Legal Characteristics

The Norwegian legal system is divided into the Supreme Court of Justice, Courts of Appeal, County and Town Courts, and the Examining and Summary Courts.

The Norwegian General Penal Code became effective in May 1902. Revisions of the code may be made, based upon recommendations of an Advisory Committee on Criminal Law (see Appendix D). Punishable acts are divided into two categories: serious crimes and offenses. These would roughly be equivalent to felonies and misdemeanors. An offense is defined as any act which does not exceed a maximum penalty of three months imprisonment. All other acts, which carry a greater penalty, are classified as serious crimes.

Ranking police administrators are part of the Public Prosecution Authority. Norway is divided into fifty–three police districts. Within each district are police commissioners and superintendents who have university law degrees. These police administrators

---

20. Translated from the thirteenth century Norwegian Frostating Law. (The ancient provincial law from Middle Norway, called Frostating Law, probably originated before the unification of Norway in A. D. 872. In the thirteenth century the law was incorporated in a general code.)

have a dual responsibility to the Public Prosecution Authority and to the Ministry of Justice (Refer to Figure 31 for a description of criminal prosecution in Norway).

Whether the court is composed of professional or lay judges is determined by the seriousness of the criminal acts. For example, in a county or town court a professional judge may be assisted by several lay judges. In a court of appeal, dealing with a criminal case, there may be three professional judges and a jury of ten members (See Figure 32 for a description of the court system in Norway).

In Norway the legal system is set up to settle grievances of a criminal or a civil nature, but in addition, there is the ombudsman. The office of ombudsman was created for military institutions in 1952. In 1962 a civilian ombudsman was introduced to protect the rights of citizens against improper governmental actions. The ombudsman is elected by parliament for four years at a time and must possess qualifications equivalent to that of a supreme court judge. His responsibility is to investigate governmental infractions and give advice based upon his findings.

Organization of the Police

The present Norwegian police system can be dated from 1866. In that year the police of Oslo were organized into separate patrol, detective, legal, and administrative sections.

The Police Law of 1936 established a national police system in Norway with control centralized in the national government. The country is divided into fifty–three police districts, each district being directed by a police chief. The districts operate independently, but in accordance with the policies and procedures of the Ministry of Justice and Police. Each chief of police must have a university degree in law. A Royal Decree of 1736 stated that any official who is to exercise judicial powers must be required to have a degree in law. In the 1887 Act of Procedure in Criminal Cases, it was established that the control of judicial powers was to be held by executive police officers. These actions, in effect, established the criteria that all executive policemen have university degrees in law.

I.

THE KING IN COUNCIL

(1) Exclusive competence: to make decision as to whether indictment should be issued and criminal proceedings be instigated against higher State officials (i.e. those appointed by the King in Council) on account of punishable acts committed in their capacity as such;

(2) Special competence: to make final decision with regard to cases where the State Director of Public Prosecutions has recommended that criminal proceedings should be waived or brought to a conclusion, in spite of allegedly sufficient evidence, cf. II (1), (c) below;

(3) General competence: (a) to make final decision with regard to other decisions by subordinate organs which may according to provisions of law be brought before the King in Council; (b) to issue general and special instructions and directives to subordinate organs in all matters relating to criminal investigation of "crimes" and "offences."

• II.

THE STATE DIRECTOR OF PUBLIC PROSECUTIONS

(1) Mandatory competence: to make decision as to whether indictment should be issued and criminal proceedings be instigated or waived with regard to:

(a) "crimes" which may, according to the penal clause in question, be punished with imprisonment for life;

(b) "crimes" directed against the sovereign rights of the State, or against its internal or external security; "crimes" directed against the Norwegian Constitution or the Head of the State; "crimes" directed against the free and unimpaired enjoyment and execution of civic and democratic rights; certain other "crimes" particularly enumerated by the law; "crimes" committed by way of printed matter;

(c) cases (regardless of the kind of "crime" or "offence" involved, and no matter the punishment laid down by the law) which must be considered to be of particularly great public concern. A decision to waive proceedings in cases of the latter kind is subject to final decision by the King in Council;

(2) Special Competence: to make decision in cases where the State Advocate has recommended that criminal proceedings be waived, in spite of allegedly sufficient evidence, cf. III (1).

(3) General competence: same powers in relation to subordinate organs as mentioned under I (3).

III.

THE STATE ADVOCATES

11 State Advocates, dispersed in 8 regional districts,
each usually covering several police districts

(1) Mandatory competence: to make decision as to whether indictment should be issued and criminal proceedings be instigated or waived, in all cases concerning "crimes" where the powers to make such decisions are not exclusively or mandatorily vested in the superior organs, cf. I (1), and II (1) above. A decision to waive criminal proceedings, in spite of allegedly sufficient evidence, is *subject to leave* from the State Director of Public Prosecutions, cf. II (2) above.
(2) General competence: same powers in relation to subordinate organs as those mentioned under I (3), above.

IV.

THE DISTRICT COMMISSIONERS OF POLICE

53 districts (each headed by a District Commissioner of Police assisted by one or more deputies), usually embracing several sheriff districts, cf. below.

(1) General competence in public prosecution matters:
  (a) to make decision as to whether indictment should be issued and criminal proceedings be instigated, or waived, in all cases involving "offences"; (b) to settle such cases by the issuing of "writs" where such procedure is possible according to law; (c) to undertake criminal investigation, arrest and seizure, subject to the provisions of law.
(2) General competence in police matters: maintenance of order, issuance of licenses, etc.

V.

THE SHERIFFS

395 districts, each headed by a bailiff.

Competence i.e.: investigation of "crimes" and "offences" and other ordinary police duties.

Figure 31. Criminal prosecution in Norway. Adapted from the Royal Norwegian Ministry of Justice (ed.), *Administration of Justice in Norway* (Oslo: Ministry of Justice, 1957), pp. 60-106.

SUPREME COURT

JUDICIAL SELECT APPEALS COMMITTEE OF THE SUPREME COURT

Final decision

A

Appeal proper directed against sentences/acquittals passed by: (1) the Court of Examining and Summary Jurisdiction, (2) the County or Town Court, and (3) the Court of Appeals (as well as against certain formal judicial decisions made by the latter court). Appeal lies with the Supreme Court; to be filed with the Prosecution Authority or the lower court in question. An appeal proper can be based only on one or more of the following alleged mistakes of the lower court: (a) mistakes in the application of rules of procedure, (b) mistakes in the application of provisions of substantive criminal law, (c) mistakes in the adjudication of evidence *outside* the question of guilt, and (d) fact that punishment imposed is too severe or too lenient. If the accused was acquitted by the lower court, he has no right to file an appeal proper unless the question of guilt was in fact decided against him. In cases tried by the County or Town Court an appeal proper cannot be based on grounds which may lead to renewed trial by the Court of Appeals, cf. col. C. In cases tried by the Court of Appeals an appeal proper cannot, to the detriment of the accused, be based on an assertion that the verdict of the jury is wrong in substance, unless such assertion is based on alleged mistakes by the presiding judge when directing the jury as to questions of the law. Time limit set for filing the appeal: usually 14 days. An appeal from the Prosecution for the benefit of the accused is not subject to time limit.

B

Appeal simple, directed against decisions of the kind mentioned under col. D below, and made by the Court of Appeals in its capacity as a court of *first instance,* lies with the Judicial Select Appeals Committee of the Supreme Court. If such decisions have been made by the Court of Appeals in its capacity as a court of *second instance,* an appeal simple to the Judicial Select Appeals Committee of the Supreme Court is only admissible if: (1) the case, by the decision of the Court of Appeals, has been dismissed from the lower court because the case does not come within the jurisdiction of Norwegian courts, or because a final decision with regard to the case has previously been made; (2) the appeal is directed against the Court of Appeals' application of procedural law; (3) the appeal concerns alleged mistakes with regard to other provisions of law; (4) the appeal concerns the obligation of certain categories of persons to give evidence as witnesses. Appeal to be filed with the Court of Appeals. Time limit set: usually 14 days.

If petition thereto is granted by the Judicial Select Appeals Committee of the Supreme Court (where such leave is necessary), the case is referred to the Court of Appeals for renewed trial (by jury).

COURT OF APPEALS

In its capacities as: (1) a trial court of first instance in more serious criminal cases; (2) a court for renewed trial of other criminal cases previously tried by the County or Town Court *a prima instantia* (in both capacities the Court of Appeals is acting as an assize court, and has the assistance of a jury of 10 members); and (3) as an appeal court proper in respect of judicial decisions, other than sentences/acquittals passed by the County or Town Court or by the Court of Examining and Summary Jurisdiction.

C

In cases tried by the County or Town Court a *petition for renewed trial by superior court* (i.e. the Court of Appeals) may be filed by either of the parties. It is prerequisite to such petition that it be, in any circumstances, directed against alleged mistakes by the lower court in its adjudication of the question of guilt. The petition cannot be based solely on an assertion that provisions of substantive criminal law have been wrongly applied. In the latter case an appeal proper would be the adequate legal remedy (See col. A). If the accused was acquitted by the lower court, he has no right to file a petition for renewed trial unless the question of guilt was in fact decided against him. His petition is *subject to leave* granted by the Judicial Select Appeals Committee of the Supreme Court: (1) if the accused was sentenced to fines only, or was given a conditional or suspended sentence for a "crime" or an "offence" of certain stated categories; (2) if the accused was in fact acquitted and the case involves a punishable act for which no more severe punishment can be inflicted than imprisonment for a period of up to 3 months, possibly in connection with other additional forms of punishment; (3) if the case involves a civil claim subject to rules of criminal procedure; (4) if the case involves theft or the receiving of reindeer; (5) if the case involves an "offence" only. Petition to be filed with the Prosecution Authority or the County or Town Court in question. Time limit set: usually 14 days. A petition from the Prosecution for the benefit of the accused is not limited in time.

D

Appeal simple, directed against judicial decisions of the lower court, other than sentences/acquittals, which cannot be contested by an appeal proper, or used in support of an appeal proper, lies with the Court of Appeals. Formal judicial decisions and rulings made during the main hearing may, however, only be appealed by the parties: (1) if the case, by the appealed decision, was adjourned, brought formally out of court, or dismissed; *or* (2) if the appealed decision concerns arrest or detention, search, seizure, impositions with regard to goods, liability to pay costs or damages, or the obligation of a third party to give evidence, take the oath or asseveration, to produce documentary or other factual evidence, or the obligation to serve as an expert witness. Appeal to be filed with the lower court, or with the Prosecution.
Time limit set: usually 14 days.

COUNTY OR TOWN COURT

In its capacities as: (1) an ordinary trial court *a prima instantia*, and (2) a Court of Examining and Summary Jurisdiction.

Figure 32. The Court System in Norway. Adapted from the Royal Norwegian Ministry of Justice (ed.), *Administration of Justice in Norway* (Oslo: Ministry of Justice, 1957), pp. 60-106.

At the local police station, the following procedure should be followed. First, the legal officer hears certain offenses, which are criminal acts of a less serious nature. The arrestee is brought before the police legal officer with the understanding that the case can be adjudicated then and there. If agreeable with the defendant the case proceeds and, if found guilty, the defendant is issued a penalty: a fine, days in jail, etc. However, the arrestee can refuse to have his case resolved by the police and has the alternative of having it brought before a criminal court of law.

There are approximately five thousand police officers in Norway, or about 1.3 policemen per thousand population. In urban communities policing is done by the regular police. In rural areas a sheriff has the dual responsibility of policing and performing civil (non–police) tasks dealing with tax collecting, maintenance of roads, and other duties. Approximately one–fourth of the total police strength is made up of sheriff's personnel. (See Figure 33 for a description of the police organization of Norway, and Figure 34 for a breakdown of the police organization of Oslo.)

The police are responsible to the District Attorneys for the investigation of crime, and to the Ministry of Justice and Police regarding standardized organizational policy and procedure.

The policeman is equipped with a rubber baton while on routine patrol. Normally the police do not carry guns, although rifles, pistols, and handcuffs are available at the police station.

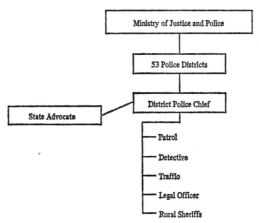

Figure 33. Police Organization of Norway.

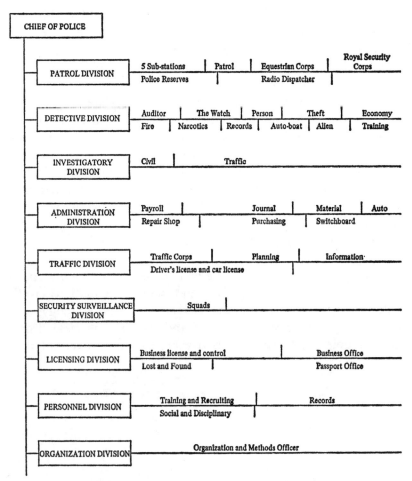

Figure 34. Organization of the Oslo police, 1968. Adapted from *Beretning om Oslo politi 1968* (Oslo: Hellstrom & Nordahls Boktrykkeri, 1969), p. 75.

In terms of recruitment, the Norwegian policemen are divided into two groups: legal officers and policemen. The chiefs of police and assistant chiefs are appointed by the King. Other personnel are selected by appointment boards or appointed by the Ministry of Justice and Police (with recommendations from appointment boards). Sheriffs are selected by appointment boards on the basis of recommendations from the city council.

An applicant for a police position must be a citizen between twenty and thirty years of age, having a high education or its equivalent, having completed military service, and being in good health. (See Figure 35 for a breakdown of the educational level of new recruits in 1968.)

Before an individual becomes a policeman he spends an initial training course of seven weeks at the local police department. He is then assigned as a police aspirant for one year in a police department in Oslo, Bergen, or Trondheim. The police cadet receives various work assignments during the year. He is then evaluated on his ability and progress, and a determination is made concerning his retention. If found acceptable, he is sent to the police training school for a ten–month course. When this course is successfully completed, he is employed as a regular policeman.

Training of the police recruit consists of the following: penal law, court procedure, civil law and special regulations, traffic control, report writing, criminal investigation, criminology, sociology and psychology, Norwegian and English, physical fitness, and self–defense. During his two years as a police recruit prior

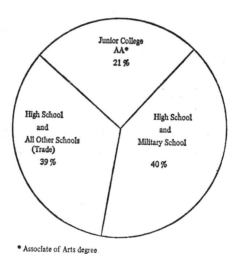

* Associate of Arts degree

Figure 35. Education level of new recruits in 1968. Adapted from *Beretning om Oslo politi 1968* (Oslo: Hellstrom & Nordahls Boktrykkeri, 1969), p. 65.

to regular employment as a policeman, he is paid less than a regular policeman.

Promotion is made by the appointment board or the King, depending on the rank to be obtained. Retirement age is based upon rank. An administrative officer with a law degree may remain on active status until 70 years of age, although he has the option to retire at sixty–seven. Whereas a constable can retire at fifty–five, other ranks must retire at sixty.

Policemen are allowed to join unions but are prohibited from striking or using a boycott by a 1959 amendment to the original Police Act of 1936. All disputes with the union are resolved through arbitration. If these negotiations fail, the conflict is settled by a special mediation council.

SELECTED READINGS
Norwegian Police Literature

General

Bratholm, A. *Pagripelse og varetektsfengsel*. Oslo: Universitetsforlaget, 1957.

Lundevall, J. *Rettsmedisin*. Oslo: Universitetsforlaget, 1966.

Midboe, F. B. *Botestraff og subsidiaer fengselsstraff*. Oslo: Universitetsforlaget, 1960.

Mjaland, B. *Etterforskningclaere*. Oslo: Politiskolen, 1964.

Osterberg, E. *Politiembetsmennenes landsforeining 1908–58*. Oslo: Webergs boktrykkeri, 1958.

Rasmussen, S. *Politimannen i Oslo, hans kamp og historie*. Oslo: Politiforening, 1954.

Rasmussen, S. *Norsk Politiforbund gjennom 50 ar. 1905–55*. Oslo: Norsk Politiforbund, 1955.

Söderman, H. *Polititroppen i Sverige; skandinavisk mellomspill*. Oslo: Gyldendal, 1946.

Valen Sendstad, F. *For lov og rett i 200 ar*. Oslo: Gyldendal, 1953.

Periodicals and Journals

Kunngjöring til politiet. Ministry of Justice and Police, Oslo.

Lensmannsbladet. Norges Lensmannslag, Oslo.

Lensmannsbetjentenes Blad. Lensmannsbetjentenes landslag, Oslo.

Norsk Politiblad. Norsfi Politiforbund, Oslo.

Politiembetsmennenes Blad. Politiembetsmennenes Landsforening, Oslo.

Politimannen. Politiets Sentralorganisasjon, Oslo.

VIII. SPAIN

Political Traits

The population of Spain is made up of approximately thirty-three million persons in a land area of about 195,000 square miles.

The present national government of Spain can best be described as a dictatorship. The national government, through its executive leadership, has dominant power in the direction of legislative, judicial, and executive behavior. The present form of government was well established at the conclusion of the Civil War (1936–1939), a dictatorship established in fact, with supreme powers of control.[21] At the death of the present dictator, political leadership is to revert to a monarchy. The monarch–elect has been pre–selected by the present dictator. It is felt by some recorders of Spanish politics that the movement from dictator to monarch would be in name only and that the substance of the present government would continue.

There is a nineteen–member cabinet and 563–member parliament at the national level. There are fifty provinces which have councils that minister to local needs following the direction of the national government.

Legal Characteristics

Spain's supreme court president and fifteen of its members are appointed by the leader of the national government. The supreme court does not hear appeals against governmental decisions.

In theory no citizen can be held by police authorities for more than seventy–two hours without being brought before an appropriate court for a legal ruling.

Spain is divided into fifteen judicial districts and each region has a high court to hear criminal cases. The courts are located in the main capital of each judicial district. There are courts of first

---

21. See the following sources for a description of Spain's governmental development: Raymond Carr, *Spain 1808–1939* (London: Oxford University Press, 1966); George Hills: *Spain* (New York: Praeger Publishers, 1970); James Cleugh: *Spain in the Modern World* (New York: Alfred A. Knopf, 1953); and Hugh Thomas: *The Spanish Civil War* (Harmondsworth, Middlesex: Penguin Books, Ltd., 1961).

instance in each province and numerous lower courts to hear petty offenses.

The structure of the Spanish court system is outlined in Figure 36.

Organization of the Police

There are three principal police forces in Spain which broadly fall under the definition of public safety. A fourth police system does exist which is devoted to undercover intelligence investigation of citizens associated with subversion of the Spanish government.

However, the purpose of this chapter is to describe the three visible police systems of Spain: (1) the Civil Guard (Guardia Civil); (2) the Armed Police (Policía Armada); and (3) the Municipal Police (Policía Municipal).

The Civil Guard is a military police system applied to civilians. There are approximately 60,000 Civil Guards. Control comes directly from the national government. The principal function of the Guard is enforcement of laws in rural areas of Spain, but it extends into major municipalities. The Guard follows the military hierarchy from private to general. Units can be found throughout Spain, based upon population and enforcement need. The

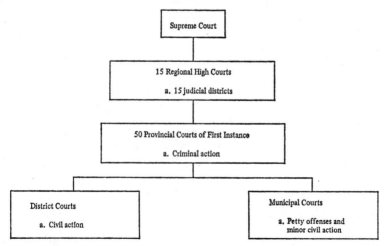

Figure 36. Structure of the Spanish Court System, 1969.

majority of the Guard patrols on foot and always in pairs. When mobilization is necessary, trucks, jeeps and army–personnel carriers of every description are available for transportation. The Civil Guard procedures and practices would be described as ruthless when compared to a democratic government's police system. Coercion, physical force, and general violence are acceptable techniques utilized by the Guard. Through it a philosophy designed to instill fear (and sometimes terror) is generated in order to secure and maintain the respect this police organization feels it should receive from the populace. Crowd control tactics are based upon military lines and the heavy use of physical force and firearms. It is not unusual to use machine guns and other types of automatic weapons to disperse civilians during the early formation of crowds.

The average Spanish citizen has a mixture of hatred and fear whenever he observes or interacts with the Civil Guard.

The Armed Police are responsible for law enforcement in the major cities and towns. The Armed Police also follow the military scheme and during a period of national emergency the organization will be activated into the Spanish Army. There are approximately 25,000 personnel in the Armed Police. There are police headquarters and sub–stations from which foot and auto patrol units are assigned. Again, all Armed Police personnel work in pairs. There is public resentment toward the Armed Police, although it is not as pronounced as that directed toward the Civil Guard. The Armed Police have attempted to develop an image that is forceful and strong, but at the same time less ruthless than that of the Civil Guard. Both police systems are responsible to the leader of the government for the enforcement of laws and public security.[22]

Unlike the Civil Guard and the Armed Police, **the Municipal Police** are responsible to the individual city, town, or village by which they are employed. Their prime police function is the regulation of traffic. The Municipal Police also have a good relationship with the local citizenry.

---

22. *Los Servicios Espanoles de Policía* (Madrid: Direccion General de Seguridad, n.d.)

There are approximately 35,000 Municipal Police in Spain. Most of these policemen are recruited from the municipality in which they are going to work. The Civil Guard and the Armed Police do not allow their police personnel to be assigned to their own areas of residency.

Training of the Municipal Police is the responsibility of the local municipality and ranges from no police instruction to an extensive training period, as in Barcelona and Madrid. In Barcelona, the training deals not only with traffic regulation and laws, but also with understanding of social norms and human behavior.[23]

The Municipal Police can best be described as a local autonomous traffic enforcement force, while the Civil Guard and the Armed Police are national military police organizations designed to maintain control of the Spanish population and safeguard national public security.

It is not uncommon to find all three police systems operating in the same municipality. On occasion organizational conflict develops over jurisdiction, communication, and particularly the underdevelopment of cooperation and coordination between police agencies.

SELECTED READINGS
Spanish Police Literature

General

Al pio Marquez, L. *Manual del Guardia nacional en funciones de resguardo marítimo*. Madrid: Marsiega, 1963.

Arnau, F. *Historia de la policía*. Barcelona: Luis de Caralt, 1966.

Carrera del Castillo, N. *Oposiciones. Cuarpo Auxiliar Femenino de la Dirección General de Seguridad. Oficios y ficheros*. Madrid: Academia Carrera del Castillo, 1963.

Cayet, J. *Manual de la policía científica*. Barcelona: Zeus, 1962.

Periodicals and Journals

Guardia Civil. Calle Costanilla de los Angeles, no. 11, Madrid.

---

23. Based upon a review of training manuals used for recruit training by the Municipal Police in Barcelona entitled *Cursos de Perfeccionamiento para mandos de la Policía Municipal*, Barcelona, 1969.

Investigación. Policía Espanola, Calle Costanilla de los Angeles, no. 15, Madrid.
Policía Armada y de Trafico. Policía Armada, Avenida José Antonio 34, Madrid.
Policía. Dirección General de Seguridad, Madrid.
Policía Judicial y Administrariva. Av. Reina Victoria 53, Madrid.
Policía Municipal. Mamón de la Cruz 54, Madrid.

IX. SWEDEN

Political Traits

The population of Sweden is approximately eight million in a land area of approximately 174,000 square miles. The political structure is best described as a constitutional monarchy, since the King does not have political power in the real sense, it being vested in the Prime Minister, Governmental Ministers, and Parliament. The national government has been flexible and steady in its historical development.

No society has undergone full modernization with greater rapidity, tranquility, and thoroughness than Sweden did. In the course of a generation, from the 1890's to about 1920, Sweden saw the rapid and simultaneous development of organized liberalism and socialism, of parliamentarianism and popular democracy, and the transformation to an industrial society.[24]

The constitution was adopted in 1809 and has been amended, on occasion, by direction of Parliament. Whereas other nations can be described as highly factionalized in terms of political partics and institutions, Sweden is best characterized by cooperation and compromise.

Parliament has historically been divided into the upper and lower houses. In 1971, however, the bicameral system was abolished and a unicameral Parliament came into effect. Its members are elected for a term of three years.

There are twelve ministerial departments, one being the Ministry of Justice, which is responsible for the police.

Although there is a high degree of political and social stability, constant change has taken place in Sweden's development. Unlike the period of turbulent Viking exploration which took place

---

24. Richard F. Tomasson: *Sweden: Prototype of Modern Society* (New York: Random House, 1970), p. 8.

from approximately 800 to 1050, Sweden's recent position of neutrality can best be summed up by this statement: "The country has never had a civil war or a national revolution and has not participated in war since 1814." [25]

Legal Characteristics

The Swedish legal system has been influenced more by old Germanic law than by Roman law. The present criminal code dates from 1734, but constant revision has brought statute changes in the penal code and has consistently reflected national social trends.

Courts are divided into Rural Courts and Borough Courts. Appeals move from the lower courts to the Courts of Appeal and up to the Supreme Court. See Figure 37 for a description and comparison of the Swedish court system.

It has been pointed out in the literature about this system and confirmed by observation, that the simplicity of Swedish law created a unique understanding of law on the part of the general populace. A book on their country's law can be found in the possession of most inhabitants of Sweden. A knowledge of basic law and individual rights is viewed as practical and is a part of the public educational process.[26]

To help maintain understanding and respect for the law, a position of ombudsman was introduced by the Constitution of 1809. The ombudsman is responsible for the inspection and investigation of civil service practices and procedures .At present there are three Commissioners (ombudsmen) who are appointed by Parliament. All public employees and agencies are required to give assistance and information when necessary to the ombudsman. The ombudsman can initiate legal action, generate public criticism of wrongful acts, or make recommendation that formal action

25. *Ibid.*, p. 17. Also see the following works dealing with Sweden: Stewart Oakley: *A Short History of Sweden* (New York: Frederick A. Praeger, 1966); Frederic Fleisher: *The New Sweden* (New York: David-McKay, 1967); Dankwart A. Rustow: *The Politics of Compromise* (Princeton: Princeton University Press, 1955); and Nils Andrén: *Modern Swedish Government* (Stockholm: Almqvist and Wiksell, 1961).
26. Refer to the study by Marquis Childs: *Sweden: The Middle Way* (New Haven: Yale University Press, 1961), p. 4.

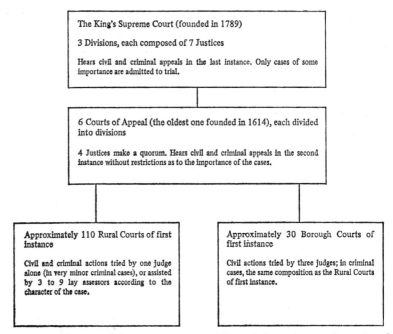

The King's Supreme Court (founded in 1789)

3 Divisions, each composed of 7 Justices

Hears civil and criminal appeals in the last instance. Only cases of some importance are admitted to trial.

6 Courts of Appeal (the oldest one founded in 1614), each divided into divisions

4 Justices make a quorum. Hears civil and criminal appeals in the second instance without restrictions as to the importance of the cases.

Approximately 110 Rural Courts of first instance

Civil and criminal actions tried by one judge alone (in very minor criminal cases), or assisted by 3 to 9 lay assessors according to the character of the case.

Approximately 30 Borough Courts of first instance

Civil actions tried by three judges; in criminal cases, the same composition as the Rural Courts of first instance.

Figure 37. The Swedish Court Ststem. Adapted from *Facts about Sweden* (The Swedish Institute, 1969), p. 24.

be taken by proper agencies of the government. The philosophy of the ombudsman is to safeguard the interests of citizens. The ombudsman will investigate complaints made by citizens or initiate an inquiry through his office. Matters regarding police personnel, policy and procedures are possible areas of inquiry for the ombudsman.

Organization of the Police

On January 1, 1965 the Swedish police were reorganized into a national police system. There are now approximately 13,400 policemen in Sweden, with 1.7 police per thousand population.

Control of the police originates with the National Police Board, which exercises authority over police forces under the Ministry of Justice. The Board consists of a National Police Commissioner, the Deputy National Commissioner and, in matters of security, a Division Head. In addition to a special Security Division, the Board is made up of a secretariat.

The Board is responsible for inspection and coordination. Its operational functions relate to the following:

1. Prevention and discovery of crimes
2. Security of dignitaries
3. Traffic enforcement affecting two or more county administrative areas
4. Investigation of crimes of an international nature, such as narcotics, alcohol, counterfeiting and smuggling

The National Police Board is controlled by a committee consisting of the National Police Commissioner, a Deputy National Commissioner, and five members appointed by the King.

Sweden is divided into twenty–three police regions. Each region is directed by a police commissioner and consists of several police districts. There are 119 police districts, each one directed by a police chief (See Figure 38 for the national structure of the police).

As the police system is centralized in Sweden, the role of the police officer is more decentralized in that he has greater decision–making power. Decisions that could only have been made by the chief of police are now being made by senior police patrolmen.

A police district is defined as having a police force of twenty or more officers. However, the majority of police personnel are stationed in the heavily populated areas of the country.

At the regional level is a County Police Commissioner. His principal responsibilities are the operational direction of the police within the county administrative area, the inspection of the various police districts, and coordination of the activities of the local police districts. In order to develop greater efficiency, special county traffic units have been created with responsibility for regional traffic control. In criminal investigation the County Police Commissioner is responsible for crimes involving several different police districts.

Within each police district is a citizens' advisory group called the Police Committee. This group is responsible for interacting with the police chief and developing recommendations on police policy and procedure. The recommendations, however, are not binding, only advisory. See Appendix E for rules governing rela-

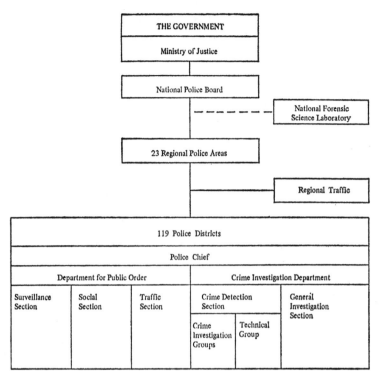

Figure 38. National Structure of the Police. Adapted from the National Swedish Police Board Information, 1969.

tions between local police authorities and police committees in Sweden.

The National Police organization is divided into five functional sections below the Deputy National Police Commissioner: (1) Department A deals with operational policing by patrol, traffic and criminal investigation personnel; (2) Department B deals with technical and training activities; (3) Department C is responsible for personnel and administrative tasks; (4) Department D deals with data processing; and (5) Department E is involved with security (see Figure 39 for a graphic presentation of the police organization).

The police utilize helicopters in traffic control, and dogs and horses during crowd control situations, or when called for by officers in the field. The entire system is supported by modern

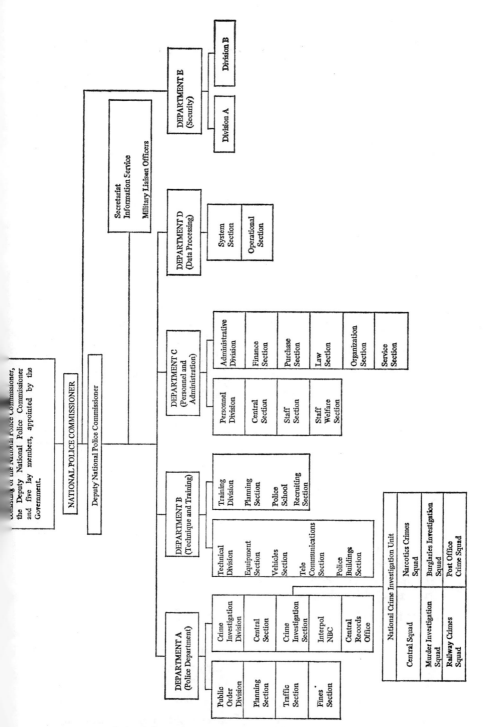

Figure 39. Swedish Police Organization. Adapted from National Swedish Police Board information, 1969.

equipment and is open to implementation with experimental devices.

Swedish police view crime prevention as a critical factor. Prevention programs have been developed by the police to make individuals more knowledgeable about how to deter robberies, auto thefts, and other burglaries. Material is presented by the news media, including radio, press, and television. The police also give instruction in the public schools regarding law enforcement subjects, to approximately 225,000 students every year.

Reference is made to Table XI for a description of policemen by work assignment and the numbers of policemen in various ranks.

TABLE XI*

NUMBER OF SWEDISH POLICEMEN

BY WORK ASSIGNMENT AND RANK—1970

Function	Number	Rank	Number
Supervision	5,800	Police Commissioners	140
Traffic	1,500	Deputy/Assistant commissioners, chief superintendents	150
Investigations	3,200	Superintendents	410
Crime prevention	850	Inspectors	1,600
Headquarters	400	Sergeants	2,900
Reserve	1,650	Constables	8,200
Total	13,400	Total	13,400

* Source: National Police Board, Sweden, 1970.

Qualifications and Training

To become a police officer in Sweden one must be a citizen, have a good character, be at least nineteen years of age, have a standard driving license, pass a medical examination, and possess minimal educational standards. Initial application is made with the district chief of police who will conduct preliminary inquiry into the capability of the applicant. If found acceptable at the district level, the application is further processed by the National Police Board. If again found acceptable, the applicant is then sent to the police school for basic training which lasts forty–three weeks. Approximately 50 per cent of all applicants were accepted for police work in 1969. Practical police experience is then obtained in the police district of Stockholm where initial assignments are made. Police training for higher ranks is also conducted at the Police College.

Policemen are allowed to hold public office in their communities and to belong to trade unions.

All promotions are made from within the ranks, except for police commissioners, who are recruited from graduates of law schools. Police commissioners attend a fifty-six week course at the Police College in Solna, which is north of Stockholm. Their training is directed at both operational and staff functions of policing.

Training at the academy and the Police College is not residential in that living accommodations are not available at the teaching institutions. Refer to Table XII for a synopsis of the training programs in Sweden.

Basic Police Training takes place over a 43-week period and includes:
1. Constable's Course I for 32 weeks.
2. Practical Work for 8 weeks.
3. Constable's Course II for 3 weeks.

The Constable's Course I provides theoretical and practical instruction, the police side being at first of an introductory nature. Later on there is a more detailed study of the functions of the police and of the legal background to police work.

The Practical Work is done in the Stockholm police district.

The Constable's Course II is designed to sum up and supplement knowledge acquired earlier, both during the first Constable's Course and during the period of practical service just completed by the recruit.

Both Constable's courses are held at the police academy and combine theoretical instruction with practical application at training stations in the Stockholm police district. Police recruits are normally trained four times a year. It is estimated that approximately seven hundred recruits participated in basic police training during 1970.

The Higher Police Course consists of ten weeks of further training to be taken three to five years after completion of the basic courses. Emphasis in this training is on general police knowledge, and the course is compulsory for all police officers.

TABLE XII

SYNOPSIS OF TRAINING PROGRAMS FOR POLICE IN SWEDEN—1970*

Subject	Basic Training	Higher Police Course	Sergeant Course	Inspector Course	Superin- tendents' Course	Commis- sioners' Course
			Regular Courses			
Introduction	X	X	X	X		X
Police Service	X	X	X	X	X	X
Supervision	X	X	X	X	X	X
Investigation	X	X	X	X	X	X
Criminal Tech- niques	X	X	X	X	X	X
Traffic	X			X	X	X
Penal law	X	X	X		X	
Special penal law (legislation on traffic, public order, foreigners)	X	X	X		X	X
Private law	X	X	X			
Legal procedure	X					
Administration & Management				X	X	X
Bookkeeping			X			
Swedish	X					
English	X					
Civics and sociology	X	X			X	X
Psychology and psychiatry	X	X		X	X	X
Medicine and first aid	X		X		X	X
Social medicine	X					X
Forensic medicine	X		X		X	X
Motoring & Traffic	X					
Office skills (type- writing, record- ing, etc.)	X					
Physical Training	X	X	X	X	X	X
Use of service pistol	X					X
Coordinated prac- tical exercises and examinations	X	X	X	X	X	X
TOTAL	43 weeks	10 weeks	12 weeks	8 weeks	15 weeks	56 weeks

* Source: National Police Board, Sweden, 1970.

The Sergeant's Course is for 12 weeks and is taken after promotion to sergeant. In addition to extending his knowledge, the course is intended to exercise the student's capacity for coping independently with various tasks associated with police duties.

The Inspector's Course is for 8 weeks and deals with administrative functions: management techniques and their practical application and police organization.

The Superintendent's Course is for 15 weeks and is designed to provide a knowledge of police tactics, management, organization of work and staff, the fiscal management aspects, and legal characteristics.

The Commissioner's Course is for 56 weeks and provides instruction for the organization and direction of police work within a police district, management at the executive level, planning and control, and personnel administration.

Other Special courses deal with investigation of specific crimes, criminal techniques, social police work, and teachers' instruction.

SELECTED READINGS
Swedish Police Literature

General

Bernhardsson, C. O. *Mordkommissionen efterlyser.* Stockholm: Medéns, 1963

Fredriksson, G. *Kriminalstatistiken och kriminologien.* Stockholm: Almqvist & Wiksell, 1962.

Hansen, C. *Malmö Polis 1874–1949.* Stockholm: Allhems förlag, 1950.

Lassen, B. and B. Hjern: *Processrätt (i utdrag).* Stockholm: Norstedt & Söner, 1959.

Söderman, H. *Skandinaviskt mellanspel.* Stockholm: Forum, 1945.

Törnqvist, W. *Pelle Barfot blir polis.* Göteborg: Förlags AB, 1960.

Zetterqvist, A. *Kriminalchefen berättar.* Stockholm: Medéns, 1957.

Periodicals and Journals

Nordisk Kriminalteknisk Tidsskrift. Statens Kriminaltekniska Anstalt, Stockholm.

Nordisk Kriminalteknisk. årsbok Svensk Polis, Inrikesdepartementet, Stockholm.

Polistidningen. Svenska Polisförbundet, Stockholm.

Stockholms Polisen. Personelltidningen, Polishuset, Stockholm 8.

X. SWITZERLAND

Political Traits

The population of Switzerland consists of approximately six million persons living in a land area of almost 16,000 square miles.

Switzerland is a federal republic with nineteen full states (cantons) and six half–states. Individual states have their own constitution, but also take direction from the federal constitution. The present federal constitution was enacted on May 29, 1874. Although revisions have taken place, modern law has taken its present style from the 1874 constitution.

Each of the states has maintained its political independence with its own constitution and legislative body. State executive power is maintained by the State Council, and legislative control is with the Grand Council.

At the federal level of government is a president, selected by members of the legislature from a special seven–man federal council. The legislature elects the seven–member council for a four–year term. The president, selected from the council, may hold the office of president for only one year. He may not serve two years in a row. The president serves as titular head of the government. The federal council serves as the executive head of state.

The legislature, divided into two houses and consisting of forty-four members selected from the states, is called the Council of States. The second house is called the National Council and is made up of two hundred elected members based upon population size.

There are four languages spoken in Switzerland: German, French, Italian, and Romansh. In some states one of the above languages is used for the most part, with the other languages dispersed within the same state. Internal conflict based upon language and ethnic characteristics does not appear to be a problem in Switzerland. Mutual respect has long been a tradition in Switzerland, based upon full equality in civil rights and a sense of respect for the preservation of individuality and ethnic identification.

There is a strong interdependency between the national central government and each of the local states. The states are further divided into communes (approximately 3,000 of them). Each commune plays a vital role in the Swiss democratic form of government. All public activity has its origin in the commune where every citizen can participate in political discussion and decision-making.

The individual commune (or administrative district) has unique autonomy and is subject to no control from the state in the use of its discretionary powers. Communes, in essence, receive the same liberties and freedoms as the individual.

Legal Characteristics

The basis of the modern Swiss legal system is the Federal Constitution of 1874. Swiss courts are divided into federal and state systems.

The highest court is the Federal Tribunal. It has twenty-six judges and twelve deputy judges elected by the federal assembly for a six-year term. The criminal section consists of individual members representing each one of the official languages. Criminal jurisdiction is further divided into federal assize courts and the federal penal criminal court. The federal assizes consider the most serious offenses; crimes of a lesser nature are considered by the ordinary federal criminal court. Appeals are made from the state courts to the federal court.

At the state level there is great variety in criminal court organization, which is really inherent in the independence of the commune and state. Broadly defined, state courts are organized according to the criminal behavior being investigated, be the offenses felonious in nature or (like misdemeanors) characterized by a lesser seriousness (see Appendix F).

Organization of the Police

Police responsibilities are shared by the federal government, the state government, and the commune. There are a total of about 6,000 state policemen and another 3,000 police at the communal level. Independence, which is so characteristic of the Swiss federated government, is retained in the style of police systems established in Switzerland.[27]

The federal constitution gives some powers to the national government, and others to the states. The national government has the basic right to legislate on criminal matters, while the states may legislate only in regard to minor criminal offenses. Criminal procedures vary with the state, but there is also a federal law of criminal procedure. A case subject to federal criminal jurisdiction may be referred to the criminal sections of the Federal Tribunal (the Federal Penal Court and the Federal Assize Courts), or it may be referred to the legal authorities of a state on the basis of a delegation of its judicial powers.

Police duties are also shared by the states and the national government, though the greater part fall to the former. In addition to rendering administrative services, the national government has a small police force (the Federal Police), implemented by the Federal Department of the Public Prosecutor. Three of the divisions serving the Federal Department of Justice and Police have police duties: (1) the Federal Division of the Public Prosecutor, (2) the Police Division, and (3) the Federal Aliens Police. Other police duties are carried out by the states.

I.

THE FEDERAL DIVISION OF THE PUBLIC PROSECUTOR is the body of prosecuting magistrates of the national government. It conducts criminal prosecutions in criminal cases tried by the Federal Tribunal (Federal Criminal Court, Federal Assizes). In many fields the Federal Division of the Public Prosecutor can oppose sentences passed by cantonal courts in connection with criminal matters. This is done by its legal department, which has other duties in connection with criminal law and procedure (legislation, execution of sentences, appeals for reprieve and so on).

The police duties and powers of the Federal Division of the Public Prosecutor are as follows:

Criminal Police: The Attorney General of the national govern-

27. The above description is from observation and correspondence with the Consulate General of Switzerland, Los Angeles, 1972.

ment, who is in charge of the Federal Division of the Public Prosecutor, directs the investigations of the criminal police in all criminal cases under the jurisdiction of the national government. For this purpose, he may employ the criminal police of the cantons or the federal police. In criminal investigation, the essential task of the federal police is to investigate offenses against either the internal or external security of the national government.

Political Police: The task here is surveillance and *prevention* of acts which may endanger the internal or external security of the national government. Here again, the national government and the cantons share the work. At the federal level, this is done by the federal police, either alone or in conjunction with the canton police forces. The federal police may also serve as a link between the Attorney General of the national government and the canton police authorities. It also does political police work in connection with foreigners. It is for the Federal Division of the Public Prosecutor to propose the expulsion of undesirable aliens and to carry out the decisions taken by the Federal Council in this field.

The Swiss Central Police Office: This office is subject to the authority of the Federal Division of the Public Prosecutor and houses the central criminal record and identification departments.

Central Offices: In conformity with international conventions, the Federal Division of the Public Prosecutor acts as a central office for the suppression of traffic in women and children, the traffic in obscene and immoral publications, currency counterfeiting, and traffic in drugs.

The Swiss Interpol (International Criminal Police Organization) Secretariat: This secretariat is also attached to the Federal Division of the Public Prosecutor. It deals with questions of general organization and administration which arise in connection with Switzerland's membership in the International Criminal Police Organization.

II.

POLICE DIVISION: The Police Division deals with the following:

A. Cases of extradition and mutual assistance in criminal matters in international relations.

B. Assistance to Swiss nationals abroad, to aliens in Switzerland, and in repatriation.

C. Matters concerning intercantonal assistance to the needy.

D. Admission of and assistance to refugees.

E. Internment of or refusal of entry to aliens.

F. Cases concerning Swiss nationality, double nationality, and stateless persons, as well as military service of persons with double nationality abroad.

G. Road traffic.

H. Matters relative to identity papers of Swiss subjects; the establishment of identity papers for those not having any, such as stateless persons.

I. Legislative work, preparation of intercantonal conventions, etc.

III.

ALIENS POLICE: The Aliens Police have the following duties:

A. The preparation and enforcement of laws relative to their work.

B. The preparation of international treaties and arrangements concerning the entrance, departure, residence, and establishment of foreigners in collaboration with the political departments. The Aliens Police must also see that these treaties and arrangements are carried out.

IV.

STATE POLICE: All police duties not expressly reserved for the police bodies of the national government (listed above) are carried out by the states. The state police forces, and the town police forces when they are autonomous, are therefore competent to investigate the great majority of ordinary crimes.

The police of each of the states have an original form of organization which is the natural outcome of historical and regional circumstances.

The total manpower strength of the state police forces, including the municipal police forces, is about 9,000.

As a general rule, state police ranks are similar to those in the Army.

As a guide, below are details of police organization in five of the principal states:

State of Zürich: The state police force is under the direction of the state police headquarters in Zürich. Its duties are the maintenance or order, traffic control, and the investigation of crime. The municipal police of Zürich, which is a large city, have similar duties. The criminal investigation department is a branch of the state police. In the city of Zürich, the investigation of crime is carried out conjointly by the state police and a special section of the municipal police. The police have great independence of action in crime investigation as compared with the judicial authorities.

State of Basel: The state police takes its orders from the department of police in Basel. The city has no autonomous municipal police. Crime is investigated by the "criminal police" of the state police force under the strict control of the state public prosecutor's department.

State of Geneva: In Geneva, as in Basel, there is only the state police under the orders of the state police department in Geneva. It is divided into *gendarmerie* (in uniform) and security police (in plain clothes). This police force carries out all police duties in the state.

State of Berne: This state police is under the direction of the state police headquarters in Berne and, in addition, there are autonomous municipal police forces in the city itself. Thus the policing of the streets is done by the state police force *in conjunction* with the municipal forces. As for crime investigation it is ensured by the "criminal police" of the state police force and, in the city of Berne itself, by the municipal "security and criminal police."

State of Vaud: The state police force, under the direction of the state's department of justice and police located in Lausanne, is composed of two different bodies: the gendarmerie (in uniform) and the security police (in plain clothes). Both are under the command of a single person. There are also autonomous municipal police forces, as in Lausanne, which have both uniformed and plain clothes police. Crime investigation is carried out by the security police, the gendarmerie and, in the town, by the Lausanne municipal police.

SELECTED READINGS
Swiss Police Literature

General

Bach, W. *Kindliche Zeuginnen in Sittlichkeitsprozessen.* Basel: Karger, 1957.

Bauer, F. *Das Verbrechen und die Gesellschaft.* Basel: Reinhardt, 1957.

Binder, H. *Die Geisteskrankheit im Recht.* Zürich: Schulthess, 1952.

Eger, R. *Berühmte Kriminalfälle aus vier Jahrhunderten.* Zürich: Verlage Scienta, 1949.

Göker, O. *La délinquance juvenile. Etude du droi matériel applicable dans le système suisse, comparé aux systèmes anglais, belge et francais.* Genève: Thèse, 1950.

Meier, F. et al. *50 Jahre Schweizerischer Polizei-Beamter.* Zürich: Verband Schweizerischer Polizei-Beamter, 1957.

Meng, H. *Die Prophylaxe des Verbrechers.* Basel: Schwabe, 1948.

Morgenthaler, W. *Letzte Aufzeichnungen von Selbstmördern.* Bern: Huber, 1945.

Mutrux, H. G. *La police modern au service public.* Genève: Radar, 1951.

Periodicals and Journals

Der Polizeibeamte/ Le fonctionaire de police/ II funzionario di polizia. La Federation Suisse des Fonctionaires de Police, Lucerne.

Revue Internationale de Criminologie et de Police Technique. Case postale 129, Genève 4.

CHAPTER 6

CONCLUSION

THE VARIOUS ATTITUDES AND METHODS of policing presented in this study reflect some type of compromise between the police organization and the society in which it functions. The level of compromise reached "cannot exist unless the community enjoys some degree of insulation from other cultures." [28] With the availability of data regarding other societies, change may take place either in the system or by the way of influences outside the directorship of the system.

The choice of change or no change is the final phenomenon of comparative research. Not that data, based upon comparative analysis, alone will produce change; these are, nevertheless, a necessary ingredient that can, and will, widen the decision–making process in police administration.

There are two issues raised in the present study: (1) the type of internal structure and job description which in their totality describe the police organization; and (2) personnel development in the areas of recruitment, training, and promotion.

Departmental policy regarding specific issues must fit the cultural confinements of individual societies in shaping answers to specific problems. [29] Solutions to particular questions will benefit from the cross–cultural comparative method by "borrowing methods without borrowing intentions." In order to be effective, changes "must be tempered so they will blend into the local cul-

28. John W. Gardner: *Self-Renewal: The Individual and the Innovative Society* (New York: Harper & Row, 1963), p. 108.
29. H. V. Wiseman: *Political Systems: Some Sociological Approaches* (London: Routledge and Kegal Paul, 1967), pp. 21–46.

ture. In many instances the administrator insists on effecting change in a manner alien to the recipients."[30]

There are four ideal strategies which might take place, based upon the alignment of police techniques and community culture in dealing with police organizational change:

1. Accepted by police but rejected by society;
2. Accepted by society but rejected by police;
3. Accepted by society and police; and
4. Rejected by society and police.

The first two strategies are conflict oriented and the latter two strategies are non-conflict oriented. Since most organizations attempt to minimize conflict,[31] it is to be expected that majority acceptance or rejection will be dominant characteristics in implementing different *methods* into police systems.

The implementing of techniques from other cultures must be accomplished within the framework of present organizational and cultural behavior. To understand this phenomenon:

> . . . it is necessary to know how it differs from the comparable institution in other cultures. Only when one knows what is unique on a comparable scale can one begin to ask significant questions about causal relationships within a country. Hence, even that most particularistic of all social scientists, the historian, can learn much about American history by studying the history of somewhat comparable foreign nations at equivalent points in their development. And if this is true for the historian, then it is even more valid for the rest of us.[32]

---

30. Benjamin D. Paul: "Anthropology and Public Health" from *Some Uses of Anthropology* (Washington, D.C.: Anthropological Society of Washington, 1965), pp. 49–57.
31. Daniel Katz and Robert L. Kahn: *The Social Psychology of Organizations* (New York: John Wiley & Sons, Inc., 1966), pp. 89–94.
32. Seymour Martin Lipset: *The First Nation* (New York: Basic Books, Inc., 1963), p. 348.

APPENDICES

APPENDIX A

INTRODUCTION TO THE DANISH CRIMINAL CODE [1]

THE DANISH CRIMINAL CODE of April 15, 1930 went into effect on January 1, 1933. It superseded the Criminal Code of 1866 which had long proved inadequate. Work preparatory to a reform of the Criminal Law began about 1905 with—*inter alia*—the setting up of a Criminal Law Commission. In 1912 the Commission published a report in the form of a first draft for a (new) Criminal Code. This draft was examined and criticized by Professor Carl Torp. His own report, in the shape of a second draft code, appeared in 1917. Finally, a new Commission, of which Professor Torp was a member, studied both drafts and published in 1923 a third draft of the Criminal Code. Between 1924 and 1930 the Ministry of Justice and Parliament examined the abundant material contained in these three drafts, in the Records of Proceedings of the Danish Association of Criminalists, and in other technical publications. It can well be claimed, therefore, that a most thorough juridical preparation preceded the new Act of 1930, which was essentially based on the second and third drafts of the criminal code.

In form, the Code is drawn up on the lines usually followed in the continental criminal codes. It is divided into a General Part, dealing with the general principles of liability, attempts, complicity, the system of penalties, and other measures; and a Special Part, defining particular crimes.

The **Special Part** of the Criminal Code is comprised of only a selection of all offenses punishable in Danish law. The field, covered broadly, corresponds to the range of offenses indictable under English law. Most petty offenses are dealt with in other acts—

---

1. *The Danish Criminal Code* with an Introduction by Professor Knud Waaben, University of Copenhagen (Copenhagen: G. E. C. Gads Forlag, 1958), pp. 7–19. Translated in part and here reprinted by permission of the publisher.

particularly in legislation passed in recent years for the regulation of commerce, road traffic, public health, customs duties, taxation and the like. The Criminal Code is primarily concerned with those types of offense which have been known from time immemorial and which are of such gravity as to make it natural to charactirize them as crimes: offenses against the State and the public authorities, offenses against property, forgery, arson, offenses of violence against the person, and so on. The individual provisions of Chapters XII–XXIX will show to what extent the various provisions of Danish law correspond to the felonies and misdemeanors known in English law. In practice, of course, a small group predominates.

Of all types of offenses, those in Chapter XXVIII of the Criminal Code are of the greatest importance. This Chapter covers all offenses against property which are characterized by a willful and unlawful transfer of property—*i. e.*, a gain for the perpetrator and a corresponding loss for the victim in the offense. The description of these offenses is on the whole much simplified, as compared with the Criminal Code of 1866. For example, no distinction is made between different types of theft, but sections 285 through 287 give the courts a rather wide latitude in assessing the gravity of a theft.

Cases concerning violation of the Criminal Code are, as a general rule, tried by a court of first instance, consisting of a professional judge and two lay judges. The defendant or the prosecutor may appeal to one of the two High Courts sitting with three professional judges and three lay judges. Appeal to the Supreme Court as a third instance may take place only by special permission, granted by the Minister of Justice. However, the Supreme Court is bound by the fact–finding of the High Court. A more summary trial by the court of first instance, without the cooperation of lay judges, may take place when the accused has made a full confession. A small number of cases concerning grave offenses (in particular homicide) are heard by a High Court sitting with a jury.

Insofar as the **General Part** of the Code is concerned, particular mention should be made of the penalties and other measures applied to offenders. First, however, some observations seem called for on the principles of criminal liability.

The Criminal Code does not provide exhaustive rules governing the objective and mental (subjective) elements in criminal liability; though, in its essential points, the system in force is defined or implied. Thus, it appears from section 1 that the maxim *nulla poena sine lege* is laid down as a fundamental principle in Danish law. Provisions on the plea of necessity, etc. are laid down in sections 13 and 14. Section 15 fixes the minimum age of criminal responsibility at fifteen years; and sections 16 and 17, which are discussed in detail below, deal with the legal consequences of mental abnormality.

As it appears from section 19, liability to punishment is subject to the existence of a form of "subjective guilt." As in the other Scandinavian countries and in Germany, the doctrine of *mens rea* in Danish law is defined somewhat differently than in English law. It is assumed that the subjective connection (relation) to an *actus reus* will usually take the form of *dolus* (intention), or of *culpa* (negligence), or of *casus* (accidental occurrence). In principle, an offense which cannot be described as intentional, and which is not due to negligence, is therefore not punishable. So-called absolute "liability" is little known in Danish law. The question whether a certain legal provision requires intention, or only negligence, is decided under section 19 of the Criminal Code: as regards the Special Part of the Criminal Code, intention is required, unless negligence is expressly mentioned in the text (e.g., sections 182, 226, 241); in the special legislation, on the other hand, negligence is punishable unless the liability is expressly confined to intentional offenses.

A description of the system of *penalties and other measures,* prescribed in the General part of the Criminal Code, would be incomplete without some account of the historical background of the Code itself.

At the end of the nineteenth century penalties based on deprivation of liberty (imprisonment or detention) were chiefly relied upon for the prevention of crime. Under the Criminal Code of 1866, these penalties were imposed in various forms, but there was little provision for measures of a reformatory—or rehabilitative—character. The view that the deterrent effect of punishment is what counts most in putting down crime, was generally accepted. It was thought that the fight against crime might risk being lost if society, instead of imprisoning the offender to show disapproval of the offense, were to impose some measure (or penalty) related to the special circumstances of the individual case. Generally, the personality of the offender evoked little interest.

With the turn of the century other views began to prevail. These were evident in the adoption by a number of countries of the "suspended sentence." The Danish Criminal Law was amended in that direction in 1905, the amending act being especially significant historically in that provision was made therein for supervisory and other care of the offender. The International Association of Criminalists—founded in 1888 by Van Hamel of Holland, Von Liszt of Germany, and Prins of Belgium—became a motivating force in the field of reform. Carl Torp (of Denmark) effectively advocated the adoption of the Association's programme in his own country; thus it was largely due to the authority of his name that, in the drafting of the New Code, every effort was made to include provisions enabling the principle of sanction to be adjusted to the individual offender.

The Criminal Code of 1930 maintained deprivation of liberty as the primary legal consequence (of criminal behavior); in practice, however, this was applied along more modern lines—*inter alia,* through a simplification of the types of penalty and through the introduction of rules for release on parole. At the same time, consideration was given to certain categories of offenders for whom special forms of treatment ought to be available: young offenders, mentally abnormal persons, persistent offenders, alcoholics, etc. The considerations underlying this development may briefly be expressed in the following way: the deterrent effect of the penalties involving deprivation of liberty is an essential factor, but its importance should not be overestimated. The fact that punishment is to some extent being replaced by other measures, or that the classic (long accepted) features of imprisonment are being blotted out, implies no weakening in the fight against crime. On the contrary, the offender is more likely to abstain from further crinimal activities if the measure applied bears some relation to his own personality. A non–penal sanction may well serve both as a deterrent and a means of curing or helping the convicted person, or of adding stability to his character. Furthermore, the requirement that justice must prevail in the criminal field does not mean that all offenders must be treated alike, irrespective of their age, their mental state, their need for social assistance, and so on.

A. The most important special category is that of **young offenders.** Acts committed by children under fifteen years of age are (as mentioned in section 15) not punishable, but measures of (certain steps toward) care may be taken on the part of the child welfare authorities. As for the age group from fifteen to eighteen years, a charge is brought forward in relatively few cases. The Public Prosecutor will generally withdraw such a charge, in pursuance of section 30 of the Criminal Code, provided the Authorities responsible for children's welfare exercise supervision over the offender or place him in a special institution. In this respect the Code draws upon an administrative principle of long standing, and it is highly satisfactory that progress in this century has made it possible virtually to abolish the imprisonment of offenders under the age of eighteen.

Young offenders, between fifteen and twenty-one years of age, at the time of their offense, may be committed to a training establishment called youth prison (section 41). Here provisions for the Criminal Code have been influenced by the English Borstal system. An effort has been made to adopt the basic characteristics which in England account for the peculiar status of the Borstal system as the alternative to the ordinary prison. The chief (and original) institution is housed in a former country house called "Sobysogaard." It has excellent facilities for general education and vocational training. A second youth prison was established in 1954. There is no institution for girls. In actual practice, offenders under the age of seventeen are rarely sent to a youth prison. The sentence is indeterminate, the term being between one and three years; in the case of recommitment because of non–observance (violation) of the conditions for release on license, the term may be extended to a total of four years (section 42).

B. Sections 16 and 17 of the Criminal Code deal with the important subject of the criminal responsibility of **mentally abnormal persons.** The system, as applied in actual practice, has proved fully adequate. It permits the courts—to a wider extent than do the Criminal Codes of most other countries—to order special treatment (for the defendant) in lieu of punishment. In addition, the provisions of the Code have stimulated close cooperation between the legal profession and the psychiatrists being consulted, and furthermore have largely averted that conflict between "legal" and "medical" views which arises so easily in this particular sphere.

The principal guideline is found in section 16, dealing with the most pronounced states of mental abnormality—in particular *insanity* and *pronounced mental deficiency.* It is primarily for the psychiatrist to say whether, at the time the offense was committed, the condition of the accused was of that nature. It has not been accepted, however, that the courts should be bound to exempt the offender from punishment where according to the medical report there is a case of, say, insanity. Under section 16, impunity also depends upon the answer to the question whether the defendant has been "irresponsible," which is a question for lawyers rather than doctors to answer. The term "irresponsible" was not intended to indicate a clearly defined, essential characteristic of the abnormal personality, and the Criminal Code imposes no rigid theoretical construction on the controversial concept of "irresponsibility." The term is used in order to emphasize that the final decision rests with the Court. If the evidence as to "insanity" so warrants, the Court *may* deem the accused to be "responsible" and punish him. This has been done in practice in some cases, in particular where persons who have committed financial frauds have been insane (e.g., suffering from a psychotic depression), but not so affected by the mental disease as to have been unable to carry on their business and in this connection make financial dispositions. In the vast majority of cases, however, the courts hold the accused to be irresponsible if the psychiatrists have diagnosed a mental disorder medically amounting to insanity. Persons who are pronounced "mentally deficient" are always deemed to be irresponsible.

In connection with insanity, section 16 also mentions "similar conditions." This addition means that the possibility of exempting a condition is one of "defective development, or impairment or disorders which in medical language are termed psychoses." Certain conditions falling outside this concept, but which have had a quite similar influence on the judgment and power–to–act of the person concerned, may justify exemption from criminal responsibility. In practice, however, this rarely occurs.

An important supplement to section 16 is found in a provision contained in section 17 (1). The section refers to persons whose more permanent condition is one of "defective development, or impairment or disturbance of their mental faculties." While section 16 is applicable also to abnormal conditions of short duration, provided they were present at the time the offense was committed, section 17 requires that the condition shall be of some duration. Among the conditions covered by section 17 (but not by section 16) the most important are *ordinary mental deficiency* and *psychopathy*. Here, too, it is for the psychiatrists to find out if such a condition exists. The court has, however, to decide whether the accused may be considered "susceptible of influence through punishment." The question as to whether the mental abnormality shall justify exemption from punishment is thus decided by the court. According to court practice, not only should the influence a punishment may have on the offender be taken into account, but other circumstances as well (should be considered important). If a psychopath has committed willful homicide, a heavy prison sentence will often be preferred for reasons of general prevention. If, conversely, a psychopath has committed a trifling offense, he will be sentenced to a short term of imprisonment because, in such cases, it is considered undesirable to submit the offender to the indeterminate sentence of detention in an institution for psychopaths. On the whole, however, the courts have made extensive use of section 17 and thus avoided the application of penalties which would be inappropriate to psychically abnormal persons. Also subject to exemption from punishment under section 17 are persons suffering from severe neuroses or from a state of deficiency owing to abuse of alcohol or narcotics;

instead the persons may be required to undergo some form of treatment likely to meet their needs.

The measures (or penalties) to be applied to persons covered by section 16 or section 17 are indicated in section 70. In the choice of alternatives facing the court the regard for public safety shall be of primary importance. As a rule, the nature of the abnormal condition (in the defendant) will justify placement in an institution. However, the court may confine itself to, say, appointing a supervising guardian, or to ordering psychiatric treatment for the individual in freedom; and, where a form of insanity has been completely cured, the court may take no measure. All in all, then, section 70 largely permits the courts to adapt the legal effect to the nature of the individual case. The measures dealt with in section 70 are indeterminate. Any alteration or cancellation of measures (against the offender) is decided by the court.

The treatment and detention of insane and mentally deficient offenders fall to the general hospital and to public welfare services. In the case of criminal psychopaths, on the other hand, a special form of treatment and detention has been provided in Denmark, in the institution at Herstedvester (near Copenhagen), or in a second institution in Jutland. It is difficult to characterize in a few words the form of treatment that is applied here. This type of treatment, which takes into account the psychopathic tendency in the individual offender, has thus far largely been in the nature of an experiment. Efforts are made to combine general psychiatric therapy and special forms of medical treatment with work training, instruction and social care. The end in view is a maturation and stabilization of the psychopathic personality. An essential feature of this particular treatment is the application of release on parole, so as to maintain contact between the offender and the officers of the institution.

C. Against **persistent criminals** two forms of indeterminate detention may be applied: workhouse (section 62) and preventive detention (section 65). These measures are not penalties in the technical sense of the term, but are alternatives to punishment. They are chiefly intended for persons on whom previous sentences of imprisonment for a definite term have had no corrective effect and who are therefore supposed to be in need of penitentiary treatment through a long period of time. In addition to this consideration, the regard to public safety clearly stands out, especially in the case of preventive detention.

Workhouse is applied to a group of persons (among others) who are not particularly dangerous, but who have shown a constant inclination to lead an anti–social life marked by criminality (more particularly through acquisitive offenses) and in many cases also by habitual drunkenness. The period of detention is not less than one nor more than five years. Most inmates enjoy a fair measure of liberty and occupy their time in workshops or in farming.

Preventive detention is imposed in relatively few cases—on an average, one or two a year. According to court practice, it is required that the criminal tendencies of the accused should have been clearly ascertained through a number of previous sentences of imprisonment. A considerable number of those detained have pronounced psychopathic symptoms. The minimum period of detention is four years; no maximum is laid down. In practice, the average term of detention has been some seven years.

D. One of the special groups of offenders who should preferably be submitted to treatment is that of **alcoholics.** Under section 73 of the Criminal Code certain groups of drink addicts may be required to enter an inebriates' home for treatment. A more lenient measure is an order made under section 72 (1) requiring the offender not to drink and not to purchase intoxicating liquor. If he disobeys this order he is liable to be dealt with in accordance with the provisions of section 138 (2) of the Code. A good many inebriates are detained in workhouses. None of these measures has proved fully satisfactory against offenders addicted to drink. During the last ten years, however, the treatment of alcoholics seems to have been brought into more fruitful paths.

It is now recognized that penal policy in this particular field has to some extent been based on a superficial view of the causes of alcoholism and of the prospects of curing it. Habitual drunkenness and the criminality attaching to it should be viewed as part of the social and personal situation of the individual, and the means of treatment should be adapted accordingly. It rarely serves any purpose to institute measures directed against intemperance as an isolated phenomenon. Treatment should consist of medical, psychological and social therapy. Attempts of this nature have been made in recent years, and the so-called *antabuse* treatment has attracted particular attention. Antabuse is a medicine invented by Danish scientists; it is taken in the form of pills which cause sickness if the patient subsequently tastes an intoxicant. The essential thing, however, is not cure in the traditional sense through the taking of the daily pill. The medicine should rather be considered as an aid to psychological and social care. The new forms of treatment are applied in freedom or in connection with commitment to prison or other institutions. It has been possible to fit them into the existing system of sanctions, *inter alia* as a condition for suspended sentence, release on parole, and conditional pardon.

E. Mention has been made above of a number of measures against **special groups of offenders.** No measure has, however, contributed so much to reduce imprisonment as the "suspended sentence," which has now been applied in Denmark for fifty years. About a third of all cases of violation of the Criminal Code result in a suspended sentence. The conditional suspension of punishment is applied in the form that is usual in continental countries: as *a suspension of the execution* of penalty. By including the imposition of a penalty, this form differs from the *suspension of sentence* that came into existence in Great Britain and the United States in the course of the nineteenth century, the most highly developed form of which is now the British probation system.

Danish law, however, is not unfamiliar with the ideas underlying probation. Under section 56 of the Criminal Code the suspended sentence may be subject to various conditions, e. g. supervision. Besides, it will be seen from section 56 (2) that importance is attached to pre–sentence social investigations, in order to ensure a careful selection for the suspension of the sentence. Both supervision and pre–sentence investigation are usually carried out by the Danish Welfare Society, a private organization which receives State subsidies. The welfare work is in rapid progress, the staff of full–time social workers being steadily increased and greater importance being given to their professional training.

F. So far, no mention has been made of the **types of penalty.** There are three ordinary penalties: the fine and the two penalties involving deprivation of liberty, viz. simple detention and imprisonment (the latter being the normal penalty in cases of acquisitive offenses, sexual offenses, arson, forgery, and a great number of other offenses under the Criminal code).[2] *Simple detention* is considered a milder form of the penalty involving deprivation of liberty. It is applied to some less grave violations of the Criminal Code (*inter alia,* certain offenses of violence) and also to infringements of special Acts (e. g. motoring in intoxicated condition). The fixed legal minimum duration of simple detention is seven days and, in practice, its duration rarely exceeds two months.

The minimum duration of the *penalty of imprisonment* is 30 days. Sentences for a term of under four months are generally served in the local prison (like sentences of simple detention); long–term sentences in the so-called State prisons. Since World War II, the Prison Administration has made great efforts to improve the State prisons and the whole treatment of prisoners. A number of open and semi–open institutions have been established with only little prisonlike atmosphere, with a rather high degree of freedom in the daily life of the prisoners, and an extensive community in instruction, employment and recreation. A large proportion of the sentences of imprisonment of more than four months are served in the open and semi–open institutions, and consideration is given to an adequate classification of the offenders by age, previous convictions, and so on. At the same time, it has been possible to restrict the use of the old cell prisons dating back to the nineteenth century. This whole development

---

2. The death penalty is provided only with respect to a few grave crimes (more particularly treason and murder) committed in time of war or occupation for the advancement of enemy interest, and in other aggravating circumstances. These provisions are not included in the Criminal Code, but are found in a special Act of 1952.

implies a trend away from the mere deprivation of liberty (incarceration) under a strict, schematic administrative system towards an individualizing treatment of prisoners with the emphasis on instruction and vocational training, psychiatric and psychological treatment and, in particular, social care (and rehabilitation) in connection with release on parole. Of course, these reforms are directly inspired by and closely related to the trend toward prison reform in other countries.

The Criminal Code is now over twenty-five years old. This is no great age for a Criminal Code; but these intervening years have been so rich in experience and ideas on penal policy that it is legitimate to ask whether the Code still affords an adequate basis for the practical work yet to be done. In all essentials, this question can be answered in the affirmative. There is no need today for any entirely new Criminal Code, but the last decade has called for amendments to particular provisions.

The need for reforms has perhaps been least evident in the "special" part of the Code. Only in one area has any major revision been necessary, and this is an area lying outside that of ordinary crime, i.e. Chapters XII and XIII of the Criminal Code on offenses against the State and the Supreme Authorities of the State. These Chapters have been amended by the Act of June 7, 1952. No radical amendments are likely to be made at any time in the near future to the legal provisions relating to the more ordinary types of offense.

It is primarily the system of penal reaction that has held the interest of Danish criminalists in postwar years. An essential feature of the reform efforts in this field is that they have largely been inspired by collaboration among the various Scandinavian countries. By 1939 Sweden had already commenced a gradual revision of its penal legislation. Denmark and Norway followed suit when, after 1945, it became possible to think of reforms in these countries. Problems of common interest have been discussed at the meetings and congresses of the associations of Scandinavian criminalists, and at conferences which have been held at regular intervals since 1948 at the urging of succeeding Scandinavian Justice Ministers.

In 1950 a permanent *Criminal Law Commission* was charged with considering and making recommendations toward a partial reform of the Criminal Code. The President of the Commission is Professor Stephan Hurwitz. Among the tasks that have been entrusted to the Commission are two which should be singled out for special mention.

In 1950 the Commission submitted a Report on the forfeiture of civil rights as a consequence of punishment. On the basis of this Report an Act was passed in 1951 amending *inter alia,* the text of sections 78 and 79 of the Criminal Code. Formerly, convicted persons were largely precluded from exercising the rights that normally belong to citizens. This deprivation would often result in the penalty of imprisonment for those individuals being, in point of fact, followed by a long-term additional punishment consisting in loss of franchise, of the right to trading licenses, game licenses, and so on. The essence of the new Act is that, normally, punishment shall not entail such social disqualification. As will be seen from sections 78 and 79 of the Criminal Code, this principle has been somewhat modified; on the whole, however, convicted persons are given a less favored position in society than non–convicted persons only where this may be justified from rational considerations of penal policy.

Furthermore, in 1953, the Criminal Law Commission submitted a Report on suspended sentences. The proposals made by the Commission have not yet resulted in any amendment to the legal provisions. If the general lines of the proposals are followed, however, the provisions of Chapter VII of the Criminal Code will be somewhat changed: the end in view is a further development of the application of supervision and similar requirements, with the result that ultimately there may well be a system very much like the English probation system.

The trend of penal legislation depends on a variety of factors. In most countries a contrast between two tendencies in penal policy is obvious. Many criminalists are strongly in favor of a more extensive use of social, educational and medical treatment of offenders. Others are more inclined to stress the deterrent effect of punishment, advising caution in the application of measures likely to reduce the severity of the penal reaction. The opinion of the general public is usually strongly in favor of the latter thesis and suspicious of reforms that seem to err in the direction of leniency. In Denmark, too, there may be different opinions as to the measures to be applied; on the whole, however, there has been no difficulty in following a (median) line of policy which increases the possibilities of individual treatment and rehabilitation on the one hand, while it avoids sudden departures from the traditional course on the other.

Fortunately, the general trend of crime since 1945 has not placed major obstacles in the way of legislative and administrative progress. The crime rate rose sharply during the war, but since the end of the war the number of offenses in proportion to the population has on the whole been declining. Whatever will be the future conditions of penal policy, its further development will in all probability follow the trend indicated by the Criminal Code of 1930. New experience will be gained and proposals of reform will be critically examined, . . . with a view to finding out whether the necessary financial, personal and institutional resources can be provided. International cooperation may also greatly contribute to this development. Our present system includes elements which are clearly the result of national experience, but also elements which are quite as obviously taken from a foreign pattern.

In the Danish Criminal Code here presented in English translation, there will probably not appear to be any codification of epoch–making or sensational theories for the prevention of crime and the treatment of offenders; this is probably self–evident (obvious) from remarks made so far in this summary. On the other hand, you may find that the Code has made a major contribution to the international literature in this field by showing a system based on efforts to create a happy combination of tradition, national experimentation, and foreign patterns.

APPENDIX B

ABSTRACT OF THE NEW POLICE INSTRUCTIONS
(New Police Act of 1829)[3]

T HE OBJECT TO BE ATTAINED is the prevention of crime. The absence of crime will be considered the best proof of the efficiency of the Police.

The Metropolitan Police District is at present formed into five divisions. The number of men in each is the same, but their distribution is guided by local circumstances. Each division, marked by a name and number, is divided into eight sections, and each section into eight beats. The police force is divided into as many companies as there are divisions, and each company consists of 1 superintendent, 4 inspectors, 16 sergeants, and 144 police constables. The company is divided into 16 parties, each consisting of 1 sergeant and 9 men. Four sergeants' parties form an inspector's party; the whole company is under the command of the superintendent.

Every man admitted into the police force is to devote his entire time to the service; to serve and reside wherever he is appointed; to obey all lawful orders and conform to all regulations; not to take money from any person without express consent of the commissioners; at all times to appear in his complete police dress; and to pay all debts contracted by him, as the commissioners shall direct.

One half of the entire force will be on duty at night, and these will be relieved by the other half. The men who are off duty are to consider themselves liable to be called upon at all times. The sergeants call over and direct their respective parties, and report to the inspector. One inspector takes general charge of duty throughout the division and visits the men; the other remains

---

3. Extract from the *Companion to the Almanac: Or Year-Book of General Information for 1830* (London), pp. 132–138.

in the division station. The inspectors deliver a written report to the superintendent; the latter in turn reports to the office and sends all persons put in charge during the night to the offices of the police magistrates.

The superintendent is responsible for the general performance of the duties of the police within his division. He is to observe the conduct of all loose, disorderly, and suspected persons within it, making it evident to these persons that they are known and watched. Upon the sounding of any fire alarm, he is to repair immediately to the spot and take full charge of the police force. He is to give notice to fire offices, procure engines, preserve a free access for the firemen's exertions, render every assistance to (aid in) the removal of property, having it conveyed, if desired, to the nearest police station. He is also to collect all the information he can on the spot as to the cause of the fire, and direct special attention to thieves and pickpockets.

The inspector is responsible for the conduct of the sergeants and the 36 men under him. The inspector on duty at the division station is to receive all charges, entering them in a book according to a printed form. He is to enter all property brought to him, and mark the articles the instant they are received, locking them up in a place set aside for that purpose. He will take care that all persons brought under charges are securely confined. If the offense with which they are charged be only a petty misdemeanour, he may set them at liberty, taking cognizance that they are to appear the next day at the sitting magistrates' office. In case application is made to him for assistance, he will, according to the best of his judgment, render all in his power, either from the reserve party, or by calling up those off duty; but this last is only to be done in cases of necessity.

The sergeant is responsible for the conduct of the nine men under him. He is constantly to patrol his section to enforce the performance of duty by his men. Always at night he carries a (dark) lantern. In case of any felony or disturbance, he will send for such assistance as may be necessary. He will give all assistance in his power to persons applying to him. In case of fire, in the absence of the superintendent and inspector, he will act according to the instructions given for the guidance of these people.

He must notice hackney–coaches and other carriages at night, which appear under suspicious circumstances. He is to be civil and attentive to everybody, and to render every information and assistance in his power when required.

The police constable will be held responsible for the security of life and property within his beat, and for the preservation of peace and general good order during the time he is on duty. He should make himself perfectly acquainted with all the parts of his beat or section, with the streets, thoroughfares, courts, and houses. He will be expected to possess such a knowledge of the inhabitants of each house, as will enable him to render assistance to the inhabitants when called for. He will be able to see every part of his beat, at least once in ten minutes or a quarter of an hour. This he will be expected to do, so that any person requiring assistance, by remaining in the same spot for that length of time, must certainly meet a constable. This regularity of moving through his beat shall not, however, prevent his remaining at any particular place if his presence there be necessary to observe the conduct of any suspected person, or for any other good reason that shall be satisfactory to his superior. All his duty will be carried on in silence: he is not to call the hour. When he takes anyone into custody, he will immediately repair to a spot in the section, appointed for the purpose, and remain there with the prisoner until some constable comes who can take his place.

He shall not enter any house except in the execution of his duty; he will pay a particular attention to all public–houses in his beat. Under no pretext shall he enter any public–house except in the immediate execution of his duty; the publican [4] is subject to a severe fine for allowing him to remain in his house. No liquor of any sort shall be taken from a publican without paying for it at the time. If at any time he requires immediate assistance, and cannot in any other way obtain it, he must spring his rattle, but this is to be done as seldom as possible.

He will be civil and attentive to all people, of every rank and class, and be ready to give information and assistance when re-

---

4. Here the licensee of a public house.

quired; but he must not enter into conversation while on duty with anyone, except on matters relating to his duty.

He must be particularly cautious not to interfere idly or unnecessarily. When required to act, he will do so with decision and boldness; on all occasions he may expect to receive the fullest support in the proper exercise of his authority. He must remember that there is no qualification so indispensable to a police officer as a perfect command of temper, never suffering himself to be moved in the slightest degree by any language or threats that may be used. If he does his duty in a quiet and determined manner, such conduct will probably induce well–disposed bystanders to assist him, if he should require them to do so.

The commissioners may recommend him to the Secretary of State for a reward, in case of extraordinary exertions; but under no pretext is he to receive a gratuity from any person for anything relating to his duty, on pain of immediate dismissal.

In the instructions of the New Police it is particularly required that every member of the force should make himself perfectly acquainted with such parts of the Law as relate to the Office of a Constable; an abstract of his legal duties is, therefore, added to the instructions, which, as it may be of general utility, is here printed without abridgment. It should be noticed, however, that some of the directions are drawn from local Acts, applicable only to the metropolis or its vicinity. The paragraphs containing these are included in brackets.

DUTIES OF A CONSTABLE

It is intended here to state such parts of the law relating to the office of a constable as may be sufficient for the general instruction of the police force.

Each individual will bear in mind the extreme importance of making himself perfectly acquainted with this subject. It is necessary to enable him, with a due regard to his own safety, to act efficiently for the protection of the public.

At the commencement of a new establishment, it is the more necessary to take particular care that the constables of the police do not form false notions of their duties and powers.

The powers of a constable, as will appear hereafter, are, when properly understood and duly executed, amply sufficient for their purpose. He is regarded as the legitimate peace–officer of his district. Both by the common law and many acts of Parliament, he is invested with considerable powers, and has imposed on him the discharge of many important duties.

He is, in many cases, authorized and required, in the execution of his office, to arrest a party, charged with or suspected to be guilty of some offense; to enter a house, in pursuit of an offender—to quiet an affray—to search for stolen goods—to take possession of goods suspected of having been stolen.

It therefore becomes necessary that the constable should inform himself in what cases he ought so to interfere; and what legal powers he possesses to effect the object in case he meets with resistance. To assist the police constables in the discharge of their duties, the following observations are prepared for their attentive perusal.

We shall begin by showing him for what offenses of more ordinary occurrence a party may be arrested and taken into custody. With this object, offenses may be divided into —

Felonies and Misdemeanours

Murder, house–breaking, robbery, stealing, picking pockets, receiving stolen goods knowing them to have been stolen, assaulting anyone with intent to rob, setting fire to any church, house, or other buildings, are some of the principal felonies, besides a great many more too numerous to be inserted here.

Persons guilty of any of these offenses are called felons.

Smaller offenses, such as common assaults, affrays, and riots, are called misdemeanours.

As it is more important to prevent and punish the commission of great crimes, than of the lesser offenses, the constable has a greater power in cases of felonies than in those of mere misdemeanours.

But the first duty of a constable is always to prevent the commission of a crime.

We shall therefore now show him what power he has to arrest a party, whom, from his situation and character, the law judges to be likely to commit some felony.

The constable may arrest one whom he has just cause to suspect to be about to commit a felony. Thus when a drunken person, or a man in a violent passion, threatens the life of another, the constable should interfere and arrest.

He should arrest any person having in his possession any picklock–key, crow, jack, bit, or other implement, with intent feloniously to break into any dwelling–house, warehouse, coach–house, stable, or out–building; or any person armed with any gun, pistol, hanger, cutlass, bludgeon, or offensive weapon, or having upon him any instrument with intent to commit any felonious act.

Every person found in any dwelling–house, warehouse, coach–house, out–house, or stable, or in any enclosed yard, garden, or area, and being there for any unlawful purpose, may be arrested.

In each of these cases the constable must judge, from the situation and behaviour of the party, what his intention is. In some cases no doubt can exist: as when the party is a notorious thief, or acting with those who are thieves, or when the party is seen to try people's pockets in a crowd, or to attempt to break into a house, or to endeavour to carry off any property secretly from another. The constable will not act hastily, in case the intention is not clear, but content himself with watching closely the suspected party that he may discover his design.

The constable must arrest anyone whom he sees in the act of committing a felony; or anyone whom another positively charges with having committed a felony; or whom another suspects of having committed a felony, if the suspicion appears to the constable to be well founded, and provided the person so suspecting go with the constable.

Though no charge be made, yet if the constable suspect a person to have committed a felony, he should arrest him; and if he has reasonable grounds for his suspicion, he will be justified, even though it should afterwards appear that no felony was in fact committed. But the constable must be cautious in thus acting upon his own suspicions.

Generally, if the arrest was made discreetly and fairly, in pursuit of an offender, and not from any private malice or ill–will, the constable need not doubt that the law will protect him.

If, after sunset and before sunrise, the constable shall see any one carrying a bundle, or goods, which he suspects were stolen, he should stop and examine the person, and may detain him. Here also he should judge from circumstances (such as the appearance and manner of the party, his account of himself and the like) whether he has really got stolen goods, before he actually takes him into custody.

The constable must make every exertion to effect the arrest, and the law gives him abundant power for the purpose. If the felon or party accused of felony flees, he may be immediately followed wherever he goes. If he takes refuge in a house, the constable may break open the doors, if necessary, to get in, first stating who he is, and his business. But the breaking open of outer doors is so dangerous a proceeding, that the constable never should resort to it except in extreme cases, and when an immediate arrest is necessary.

There are some cases, in which a constable may and ought to break into a house, although no felony has been committed, when the necessity of the case will not admit of delay, as when persons are fighting furiously in a house, or when a house has been entered by others with a felonious intent, and a felony will probably be committed unless the constable interfere and there is no other means of entering. Except in such cases, it is better, in general, that the constable should wait till he has a warrant from a magistrate for the purpose.

If a constable finds his exertions insufficient to effect the arrest, he ought to require all persons present to assist him, and they are bound to do so.

If a prisoner should escape, he may be retaken, and, on immediate pursuit, the constable may follow him into any place or any house.

In cases of actual breaches of the peace, as riots, affrays [brawls], assaults, and the like, committed within the view of the constable, he should immediately interfere (first giving public notice of his office, if he be not already known), separate the combatants, and prevent others from joining in the affray. If the riot, etc. be of a serious nature, or if the offenders do not immediately desist, he should take them into custody, securing also the principal instigators of the tumult, and do everything in his power to restore quiet.

He may arrest any one assaulting or opposing him in the execution of his duty.

If a person forcibly enters the house of another, the constable may, at the request of the owner, turn him out directly. If he has entered peaceably, and the owner requests him to go out, and unless he does so, he should turn him out: in either case using no more force than is necessary for that purpose.

When the offense has not yet been committed, but when a breach of the peace is likely to take place, as when persons are openly preparing to fight, the constable should take the parties concerned into custody. If they flee into a house, or are making preparations to fight within the house, the constable should enter the house to prevent them, and likewise take the parties into custody. Should the doors be closed, he may break them open, if admission is refused, after giving notice of his office, and his object in entering.

If any party threatens another with immediate personal violence, or offers to strike, the constable should interfere, and prevent a breach of the peace. If one draws a weapon upon another, attempting to strike, the constable should take him into custody. If persons are merely quarreling or insulting each other, the constable has no right to take them into custody, but should be ready to prevent a breach of the peace.

The constable ought to arrest and take before a justice any person walking about the streets and exposing to view in the street any obscene print or exhibition; or any person willfully, openly, and obscenely in any street or place of public resort exposing his person, with intent to insult any female.

The constable cannot, in cases of misdemeanour, arrest a party after the matter has happened, upon the charge of another; though if another delivers to him a person whom he charges with having committed such a breach of the peace, the constable is bound to take charge of him.

If a party, charged with a misdemeanour, escapes out of custody, he may be pursued immediately anywhere. If he take refuge in a house, the doors may be broken open after demand of admission, and after notification by the constable of his office and object in coming.

After the arrest the constable is in all cases to treat a prisoner properly, and impose only such constraint upon him as may be necessary for his safe custody.

It is always desirable to take the prisoner as soon as convenient before the sitting magistrate, who will dispose of the case. At night he is to be taken to the division station or, in cases of necessity, to the nearest place of safety.

The constable is bound to follow the directions contained in a warrant, and to execute it with secrecy and dispatch; the power given to him for the purpose of arresting has been already shown. If the warrant cannot be executed immediately, it should be executed as soon as possible afterwards.

The constable must execute the warrant himself, or when he calls in assistance, and must be actually present. Upon all occasions he ought to state his authority if it is not generally known, and should show his warrant when required to do so; but he should never part with the possession of the warrant, as it may be wanted afterwards for his own justification.

Upon the arrest being made, the prisoner is to be taken before the magistrate as soon as convenient. When the prisoner is brought to the justice, he still remains in custody of the constable until his discharge or committal, or until he receive the orders of the justice.

The constable may enter a house to search for stolen goods, having gotten a search warrant from a magistrate for that purpose. He should, when it is possible to do so, execute it in the daytime. If he finds the goods mentioned, he is to take them to a magistrate and, when the warrant so directs, he must take the person also in whose possession they are found: to avoid mistakes, the owner ought to be present at the search to identify the goods.

The constable has power to apprehend and carry before a justice of the peace every common prostitute wandering in the public streets or public highways, or in any place of public resort, and behaving in a riotous or indecent manner—(also) every person wandering abroad or placing himself, or herself, in any public street or highway, court, or passage, to beg or gather alms, or causing, or procuring, or encouraging any child so to do, all such being declared by the law to be idle and disorderly persons.

Every person wandering abroad and lodging in any barn or outhouse, or in any deserted or unoccupied building, or in the open air, or under a tent, or in any cart or waggon, not having any visible means of subsistence, and not giving a good account of himself or herself; every person wandering abroad and endeavouring, by the exposure of wounds or deformities, to obtain or gather alms; every person going about as a gatherer or collector of alms, or endeavouring to procure charitable contributions of any nature or kind, under any false or fraudulent pretence; every person playing or betting, in any street, road, highway, or other open or public place, at or with any table or instrument of gaming, at any game or pretended game of chance in the cases; just mentioned, the constable has, by law, power to arrest. Special directions will be given for his guidance by his officers, in the foregoing and in similar cases.

If any carter, drayman, carman, waggoner, or other driver, shall ride upon his cart, dray, car, or waggon, in London, or within ten miles thereof, not having some other person on foot, to guide the same, he may be stopped, apprehended, and carried before a magistrate as soon as may be convenient. If the driver of any carriage shall, by negligence or willful misbehaviour, interrupt the free passage of his Majesty's subjects, he may be apprehended and conveyed before a justice. Also, if the coachman, guard, or other person having the care of any coach, or other carriage, shall by intoxication, or wanton or furious driving, or any other willful misconduct on the public highway injure or endanger any person, he may be apprehended.

It is lawful for any man belonging to the police force, during the time of his being on duty, to apprehend all loose, idle, and disorderly persons, whom he shall find disturbing the public peace, or whom he shall have just cause to suspect of any evil designs, and all persons whom he shall find, between sunset and the hour of eight o'clock in the forenoon, lying in any highway, yard, or other place, or loitering therein, and not giving a satisfactory account of themselves, and to deliver any person so apprehended into the custody of the constable appointed under this act who shall be in attendance at the nearest watchhouse, in order that such person may be secured until he can be brought before a justice of the peace, to be dealt with according to law; or may give bail for his appearance before a justice of the peace, if the constable shall deem it prudent to take bail.

No shop, room, or place for the sale of ready-made coffee, tea, or other liquors, shall be kept open after 11 o'clock at night, during any part of the year; nor opened before four in the morning between Lady–day and Michaelmas, or before six in the morning between Michaelmas and Lady–day.[5]

If any such are open, or being shut, if any person during the said hours shall be found therein, except the persons dwelling there, or having lawful excuse for being there, master, mistress, waiter, or other person having care or management of such shop, etc., the constable should make complaint, next day, to the sitting magistrate.

Any one blowing any horn, or using any noisy instrument in the streets, for the purpose of hawking, selling, or distributing any articles whatsoever, may be apprehended.

The following cases are cases of nuisance; in which it is desirable that the constable should only ascertain the party offending, and take the means of finding him afterwards, and report the case to the superior officer, when directions will be given him for his further guidance:

If any person in any public street or place beats or dusts carpets, or drives any carriage for the purpose of breaking, exercising or trying horses; or shall ride any horse for the purpose of trying or showing it for sale, in such a manner as to cause danger, or great annoyance to passengers; or throws any ashes, dirt, rubbish, dung, or any filth upon the carriage or footway; or shall slaughter

5. Between March 25 (Lady Day) and September 29 (Michaelmas) before 4 a.m., and before 6 a.m. between September 29 and March 25. Lady Day was celebrated in the Christian Church as the Feast of the Annunciation (the announcement made by the angel Gabriel to the Virgin Mary of the incarnation of Christ). Michaelmas is the Feast of St Michael (mentioned in Scriptures as the helper of the Church's armies against the heathen).

or cut up any beast, swine, or sheep, so near any public street that any blood or filth shall flow upon the pavement; or rolls or drives upon the footway of any street any waggon, cart, or other carriage, or wheel a wheel–barrow or truck, or any cask or barrel, or rides or drives any horse or other beast upon any of the foot-ways; the constable may apprehend the party and take him before a magistrate; but if he know the party, or can discover his residence, it will be better that the constable should lodge his complaint with a magistrate, who will then issue a summons for the party to appear.

If any person slack or sift lime in the streets, unless he can show the consent of the Commissioners of the Pavements for so doing, complaint may be made to a magistrate.

If entrances to coal–holes and cellars are not properly secured, so as to prevent danger to passengers, complaint should likewise be made.

If any scavenger or any person sweeps or places the mud, dirt, or rubbish, in any of the drains or sewers, complaint may be made in the same way.

During or after a fall of snow, or any frost, if the occupier of any house or building does not once in every day, except Sunday, before the hour of ten o'clock forenoon, sweep and cleanse the foot–way along the front or sides of their premises, complaint is to be made.

Any person carrying in any cart through the street soap lees [dregs], night soil, slop, or filth, without having a proper covering to prevent the same from spilling into the streets, or driving any cart with such soap lees, etc., through the streets at any time between the hours of six o'clock in the morning and eight in the evening, may be taken into custody at the time, or he may be summoned afterwards before a magistrate.

If any person emptys any bog-house, or takes away any night soil from any house in the streets, except between the hours of twelve o'clock in the night and five in the morning, from Lady-day to Michaelmas, or before six o'clock from Michaelmas to Lady–day, or if any person shall put any night soil in or near any of the public streets, the constable should apprehend him im-

mediately, and keep him in confinement till he can be con-
veniently carried before a magistrate, and may take his horses,
carts, etc. to some place of security, to be kept till the decision of
the matter.

APPENDIX C

THE GERMAN PENAL CODE [6]
(1871)

THE GERMAN PENAL CODE became effective in 1871 as the Penal Code for the German Reich. Its immediate predecessor was the Penal Code of the North German Federation. This federation was the union of the North German states under the leadership of Prussia. It had strived for a unification of the laws, beginning with the penal laws. Thus, after the foundation of the German Reich, its penal code could become the Reich Penal Code with but minor editorial changes. The North German Federation Penal Code, in turn, rested largely on the Prussian Penal Code of 1851.

The contents of the code are determined by two factors. First, the formulation of the definitions and their individual construction reminds one strongly of the French Penal Code, which, especially with the French occupation after 1806, had become well known in Germany, and the modern structure of which had had its fascination for the individual German states. Second, the state's reaction to the offense in the form of punishment was deeply rooted in the German idealistic philosophy according to which punishment finds its own justification in the idea of retribution and penitence. It is, therefore, a sanction to be imposed even without any rational purpose, e. g., if there is no need for the protection of the community in the particular case. On the other hand, measures whose sole function would be the prevention of crime and (meeting) the needs of society were rejected as alien to the idea of penal law.

However, it was this latter fact which, soon after introduction

---

6. *The German Penal Code of 1871* translated by Gerhard O. W. Mueller and Thomas Buergenthal (South Hackensack, N. J.: Fred B. Rothman & Co., 1961). Reprinted by permission of the publisher.

of the code, led to demands for reforms of the criminal law. The crime statistics showed a strong rise in the crime rate, especially of professional and habitual criminality. This caused the mobilization of forces which criticized the criminal–political shortcomings of the code and which demanded a reform by realigning the code along criminological rather than dogmatic lines. The beginning of this reform movement is marked by the so–called Marburg program (1882) by F. V. Liszt, who became the founder and leader of the modern or sociological criminological school in Germany. This theory emphasized the utilitarian character of criminal law and demanded a type of state's reaction to crime which serves preventive goals in a rational manner. The thought of a purely retributive punishment was rejected, and the re–socialization (rehabilitation) of the perpetrator and the protection of society were the two principal goals posited by this theory of criminal law.

These demands found as many followers as opponents and, after a gigantic struggle of both theories around the turn of the century, the criminal–political reform of the German penal law failed.

Nevertheless, in its present form the penal code has only very little in common with the penal code of 1871. In the meantime more than sixty amendatory laws have been passed by which the German criminal law has been completely revised both as to the number and the type of definitions of crimes, as well as with respect to its criminal–political outlook. It has thus been turned into a mixture of styles. However, this alone cannot properly lead to any fundamental attack against its orientations and the legislative decisions embodied therein. Nevertheless, movements are afoot for the creation of a new German penal code, and these, therefore, can be explained only by the hope of obtaining a penal code which is oriented according to uniform principles. Criminal–political considerations are of minor importance in today's reform.

I.

The structure of the penal code corresponds with that of most other European penal codes. It begins with its General Part in which all basic doctrines and provisions are detailed which are

applicable to every offense, regardless of its type, whether robbery, fraud, murder or forgery. The questions covered by these
provisions, in other words, are to be decided in an equal manner
regardless of the crime involved, e. g., the problem of incapacity
(Sec. 51), the punishment of accessories (Secs. 48, 49), the attempt (Sec. 43, et seq.), the applicability of the law within the
territory and abroad (Sec. 3 et seq.) etc. There then follows the
Special Part, containing the definitions of the various crimes.
Here we detect a certain systematic scheme of division in accordance with the interest protected, i. e. whether the deed is directed
against the community at large and the state, or whether it is
directed against the individual. The Special Part begins with
treason and other felonies against the state. There follows de-
famation, homicide, assault and battery, and offenses against
property. These criteria have not always been equally determina-
tive, and within the two groups an order is hardly detectable. It
was with special reference to this point that the code has been
criticized repeatedly for its lack of a clear, plausible and systematic order in the Special Part.

In its subdivisions of crime the German Penal Code follows the
model of the French *Code Pénal* in differentiating between felonies, gross misdemeanors and petty misdemeanors in accordance
with the seriousness of the offense (Sec. 1). Only the felonies
and gross misdemeanors are combined and treated jointly in the
classified divisions of the Special Part; all petty misdemeanors are
separately appended thereto in Chapter 29, which has no com-
parable internal order. In view of the fact that, on the whole, in
the case of these petty misdemeanors we are not dealing with
true criminality but only with more or less minor and non–stig-
matizing violations of the external order of a community, there
have been repeated demands for their entire removal from the
code and for restriction of the penal code to true criminality in
the form of felonies and gross misdemeanors. The new draft code
which has just been prepared by lawyers from all branches of
the profession does exactly that.

II.

Every penal code occupies itself with two major problem com-

plexes: first of all its task consists of describing that human behavior which is to be punishable, i. e. to create the prerequisites
under which the court must impose punishment. For that purpose
it has to posit the definitions of the various crimes, thus advertis-
ing to the general community and to the court what is prohibited
and punishable. Second, it is the task of a criminal code to determine and publicize the reactions which follow the commission
of crime. These reactions no longer consist solely of retributive
punishments. The modern criminologist knows that he must operate with a second type of reaction as well: measure of safety
and rehabilitation, conceived in order to cater to the community's
need for freedom from criminal depredations.

Within the scope of this introduction we must restrict ourselves
to the basic decisions which the German penal law has made on
these two problem complexes.

Within the sphere of the doctrines applicable to all offenses
regardless of the type of crime involved, we find the following
prerequisites of criminality.

1. First of all there must be human conduct as an object of
evaluation in terms of criminal law. This is an important consideration in view of the fact that human motions without participation of the will are mere spasms as we find them for example in
the case of the tumbling of a completely intoxicated person, movements during sleep, or in the case of epileptic fits. If there is any
such exceptional spasm, etc., we would lack the object requisite
for evaluation in terms of the law, because the legal order dis-
approves only conduct which is the product of the human will
and thus a rational emanation of man's personality. Anything
which is not the product of the human will does not deserve the
blame of the law.

2. In order to be relevant for purposes of the criminal law, this
human conduct must fulfill one of the definitions of the penal
code. That means, we must be able to bring the concrete characteristics of this conduct within the prerequisites of the definition of the penal law which threatens punishment for just this
type of conduct. It is the essential function of this standard of
conduct to grant the perpetrator the guarantees of the rule of

law, and it supposes that the perpetrator has the power to walk the path of lawfulness in preference to that of unlawfulness, without having to fear that a judge will subsequently declare that to be unlawful which the penal law heretofore had not made unlawful. In its Sec. 2 the German Penal Code (*vide* also Article 103 of the Constitution) subscribes to the basic maxim *nullum crimen sine lege,* viz., that only such conduct may be punished which expressly has been declared "criminal" by penal law. This maxim prohibits the creation of criminality by judge–made law and the application of analogy insofar as the defendant derives detriment therefrom. A correlative maxim, *nulla poena sine lege,* then provides accordingly that the kind and extent of punishment must be determined by law, meaning law which at the time of the commission of the offenses described the prerequisites and consequences of the criminal act. Furthermore, Sec. 2 provides that *ex post facto* penal laws are prohibited and that a subsequent penal law is to be applied only if it derives to the defendant's benefit.

Included in the prerequisites which the individual definitions of crimes contain, there are certain characteristics of the perpetrator—e. g., the quality of being a public official, a guardian, a trustee—or characteristics of objects against which the deed is directed—e. g., a human being, a relative, wild life—as well as the qualities of the action and its other circumstances insofar as they are proscribed by the law, and insofar as the definition of the crime does not restrict itself to stating merely the causation of the prohibited result. To demonstrate the point, in the case of perjury it is part of the elements of the crime that the statement be false; in the case of forgery it is necessary that the perpetrator have manufactured a false document; while in the case of assault and battery, in the case of manslaughter and in the case of malicious injury to property, the definitional requirements are fulfilled if the prohibited result has been caused by the perpetrator's conduct.

Whenever the law demands as a prerequisite of punishment that the conduct of the perpetrator lead to a certain injury, it is then part of the definitional elements that there be causality between conduct and result. In accordance with the prevalent view, the test of this causality is the formula of *sine qua non,* or "but for."

3. A further prerequisite for punishment is that the unlawfulness of the conduct meet the definition of the code. As a rule the unlawfulness does not have to be specially determined, because the very definition of the crime is the legislator's vehicle for the determination of the unlawfulness of a given activity. Consequently, as a rule any conduct which is in accordance with the definition of this code violates the legal order. However, certain situations are imaginable in which one has to provide by way of exception that something which normally is unlawful is to be deemed lawful under given circumstances. For example, a person subject to an unlawful attack may resort to counterforce (self–defense, Sec. 53). He now acts lawfully. The same is true for the deprivation of liberty when an arrest is made by a police officer.

For reasons of draftsmanship these exceptions are not part of the definitions of the various offenses, but rather, they are treated outside the definitions of the offenses as the group of so–called "justifications." The maxim that conduct fulfilling the definitional requirements of the penal code is *ipso facto* also unlawful, thus needs a correction: although the conduct fulfills the definition of the code, it remains lawful, and therefore not punishable, if a ground of justification is present. These grounds of justification are regulated partially by the penal code itself, but partially also by other branches of the law, for example, in the civil code under which it is lawful to use the property of others if necessary to avoid danger (Sec. 904, German Civil Code). The unity of the legal order obviously demands that something which is lawful in one branch of the law cannot be unlawful in another branch.

4. Finally, it is a prerequisite for punishment that the perpetrator's conduct must be personally blameworthy. The German law here speaks of the guilt of the perpetrator. Guilt rests on a number of prerequisites.

a. First, the perpetrator must be capable of incurring guilt, i.e. he must possess capacity. This results from the function of penal law, namely, to influence and guide the human being by its prescriptions and proscriptions and to affect him pedagogically.

Obviously, the penal law cannot fulfill this task with persons who lack understanding and intellectual capacity, e. g., mentally diseased persons or infants. Hence, it is a common basis for all provisions dealing with the capacity of the human being, that the perpetrator be capable of appreciating the unlawfulness of his conduct and of acting in accordance with such appreciation (Sec. 51.1).

b. Guilt presupposes, furthermore, that the perpetrator stands in a certain psychological relation to his conduct, and this relation may appear in the form of intention or in the form of negligence. Therefore, intention and negligence are regarded as the two forms of guilt. Under either form, the deed is regarded as the blameworthy handiwork of the perpetrator.

Normally intention is required as the guilt form, i. e. if the penal law does not say anything expressly to the contrary, punishment presupposes intentional commission of the crime. Negligence suffices only where expressly so provided by law. The concepts of intention and negligence were left undefined by the code and have always been hotly debated subjects in German criminal science. "Intention" means that the perpetrator expressly desires to achieve the result of the offense or that he regards it as a *necessary* (although perhaps not desirable), or at least as a *possible*, consequence of his conduct and does not mind it. That much is regarded as no longer subject to debate and it follows from Sec. 59 (even though not very clearly), according to which the perpetrator cannot be blamed for all those circumstances which were not known to him.

To put it positively, in order to act intentionally, the perpetrator must know all those circumstances of which the specific offense is comprised.

The real debate begins with the question of whether or not, beyond this knowledge of the individual characteristics of the definition, the perpetrator also must have been aware that he was doing something unlawful. In the last few years both criminal science and the case law have moved away from the maxim *error juris nocet,* and now recognize that a true blame can be imposed only on the perpetrator's decision *against* the law and *for* unlawfulness. But there is still a debate on whether the perpetrator who lacks such an awareness of wrongdoing may be punished for the intentional commission of the crime, or, rather, whether he should be punished for the negligent commission of the crime whenever he lacks this awareness of unlawfulness because of an error for which he can be blamed, i. e., an error resting on his negligence.

The significance of this debate is the following: According to the first view the negligent error about the unlawfulness always leads to punishment since intention suffices for all offenses, while according to the second view punishment cannot be imposed for intentional criminality but, rather, only for the negligent production of the harm wherever negligence suffices. The prevalent view, especially that of the case law, has found the following solution. The perpetrator can be blamed only if he either had the awareness of wrongdoing in fact, or at least if he could have had it. In the latter case, however, intentional criminality is not precluded. Only the blame is lessened, because with respect to the awareness of unlawfulness there was mere negligence. It follows that the perpetrator will be punished as for an intentional offense; however, the punishment is mitigated in accordance with the degree of avoidability of the error.

c. Since the blame imposed upon the perpetrator rests on his decision against the law, it presupposes that the decision for action was determined not by the demands of the legal order, but rather by other motives which are inimical to the law. Such a motivation by the demands of the law, however, presupposes a situation in which these demands have their normal impact on the human being—situations, in other words, in which the legal order can expect that the human being will permit himself to be determined by the stimuli of the law. However, in exceptional cases, other factors are so powerful that in comparison the stimuli of the law lack the necessary power of determination.

The German penal law recognizes this fact, thus paying heed to human shortcomings, in the form of the so–called grounds of excuse which have in common that in certain situations of conflict the perpetrator cannot be expected to live in accordance with the requirements of the law, because other and more powerful factors have determined him to perpetrate his deed. This is especially true in the case of necessity (Sec. 54), which leaves the perpetrator without punishment if he has committed his deed in order to save himself from a present danger of life or limb to himself or one of his relatives. A collateral provision is applicable for offenses committed in the face of invincible force of nature (Sec. 52).

5. If all these preliminary demands have been satisfied, the perpetrator must be punished as the perpetrator of a completed offense. If several persons have participated in the criminal activity we meet with the forms of co–principalship (Sec. 47), or accessoryship before and at the fact (Secs. 48, 49). There is a special form of participation which found no regulation in the code itself, the so–called mediate principalship or, as it is known in American law, the perpetration of crime by innocent agent.

6. If a deed remains uncompleted, but the perpetrator has begun with the execution, he may be punished for an attempt (Sec. 43). The attempt is always punishable in the case of felonies but, in the case of gross misdemeanors, only if especially so provided in the definition of the Special Part. An attempt at petty misdemeanor always is unpunishable. According to a nearly unanimous opinion there is a punishable attempt not only if the criminal harm is lacking, but also if any one of many elements of the definition is lacking, but the perpetrator was of the opinion that it was present. Therefore, a perpetrator may be punished for attempt if he shoots at a corpse or if he attempts to procure an abortion on a non–pregnant woman whom he merely believes to be pregnant.

III.

As discussed above, in its original form the German Penal Code knew punishment only as a consequence of crime, not considering, however, penal statutes outside the code itself and also apart from certain collateral consequences, like the impounding of objects and instruments of crime (Sec. 40). These criminologically unsatisfactory conditions were subject to constant attack, especially from the quarters of the sociological penal theory which emphasized the utilitarian concept of criminal law and which demanded an individually preventive penal law. Even though these demands did not lead to a complete reshaping of the penal code, they at least succeeded in supplementing the system of penal reactions by innumerable amendments which by today have reached a generally satisfactory state. As a result of this development the system of consequences to crime in the present German Penal Code, is as follows:

1. On the level of punishments the German Penal Code knows detriments of freedom and property. Capital punishment has been abolished. There are three forms of deprivation of liberty: confinement in a penitentiary in the case of felonies (Sec. 14); imprisonment for gross misdemeanors (Sec. 16); and confinement in a jail for petty misdemeanors (Sec. 18). The division between confinement in a penitentiary and imprisonment is subject to much debate. A uniform deprivation of liberty, differentiated in its execution only in accordance with the personality of the perpetrator, is strongly demanded. Nevertheless, one clings to the old distinction because, after the abolition of capital punishment, one desires a specially grave punishment for the most severe felonies which thus advertizes the gravity of the offense to the community at large. In practical execution, the distinction between the two types of imprisonment is relatively minor. Confinement in a penitentiary, however, has the collateral effect of deprivation of certain civil and civic rights (Sec. 31 *et seq.*).

Side by side with loss of liberty there is the (imposition of a) fine which the law favors in cases of minor importance within the gross misdemeanors. The minimum amount (of same) is five thousand, the maximum ten thousand German marks (Sec. 27), but in exceptional cases the fine may exceed this maximum limit (Sec. 27a) and, under certain circumstances, may reach an unlimited amount. It may be imposed either together with loss of liberty, or by itself, but in accordance with Sec. 27b, the fine may supplant minor loss of liberty if the purpose of the punishment so permits.

Within the framework prescribed by the legislature, the actual measure of punishment depends on the gravity of the offense, although there is no specific legislative expression of this principle.

This means that punishment must always be commensurate with the unlawfulness of the act and the guilt of the perpetrator.

In this way the German penal law basically adheres to the maxim of the relation of the punishment to the crime, envisaging a punishment which may be imposed upon the perpetrator only to the extent that it is deserved by the graveness of his deed. Thus, the German penal law must be characterized as a guilt–oriented penal law in which rational and preventive considerations play only a minor role, side by side with commensurate punishment. From the criminological point of view, however, this is not a serious shortcoming because, as detailed, the German Penal Code does have its measures of safety and rehabilitation. These are separately covered under a special title.

Therefore, the basic premise on which the German Penal Code originally rested has been maintained. *The punishment is retribution for the guilt of the perpetrator, and its extent must correspond to his guilt.* The additional demands for the protection of the community and for the resocialization (rehabilitation) of the perpetrator are recognized as justified, but they may and shall be realized only side by side with the punishment, and under a completely different heading.

Thus, the German Penal Code follows the so–called dual track system which rests on the functional difference of punishments on the one hand, and actual measures (imposed) on the other. Even in the case of measures entailing deprivation of liberty there is, thus, a double reaction on the part of the court. For example, the dangerous habitual criminal (Sec. 20a) is sentenced to a punishment and, immediately after serving that sentence, he is transferred to serve a period of less rigorous detention, in so–called protective custody (Sec. 42b).

2. The catalog of measures of safety and rehabilitation may be found in Sec. 42a. These aim at various criminological goals. In some the thought of the protection of the community against the dangerous perpetrator is paramount, as for example in the case of protective custody, just mentioned (Sec. 42e), which may be imposed without any time limitation—i.e., for as long as the perpetrator is regarded as dangerous—and which, therefore, may

be called the most effective measure of safety. But in other cases the result sought by the measure is predominantly that of the resocialization of the perpetrator by training or even medical treatment—e.g., in an institution for care and cure (Sec. 42b) or in an alcoholics home (Sec. 42c). In the case of other measures, the results hoped for are more complex. For example, detention in a work house (Sec. 42d) may sometimes serve predominantly as a training period, and other times as time spent in protective custody. There are other measures besides those which restrict liberty—e.g., being prohibited to exercise a certain occupation (Sec. 421)—in cases in which the perpetrator committed his deed under misuse of his professional duties. Next, there is the enormously significant revocation of drivers' licenses (Sec. 42m), applicable in all traffic offenses, especially in the case of driving while intoxicated. Among the older measures we find, for example, the variegated forms of confiscation (Secs. 40, 245a, par. 3, 295).

All measures entailing deprivation of liberty coincide with the punishments of deprivation of liberty. But they are aimed at different criminological goals, and neither can be replaced by the other. The German penal law, therefore, did not follow the example of foreign penal codes in which preventive considerations have led to a supplanting of punishments of deprivation of liberty by *measures* of deprivation of liberty. Rather, the German law recognizes a strict functional difference between punishments and measures. This means that all deprivations of liberty exceeding the proportions of a just retribution can be imposed only as *measures*. Consequently, preventive considerations within the framework of punishment can play any role only insofar as consonant with a retributive punishment geared both to the deed and the proportion of guilt (in the offender).

3. Since 1953 there has been a third type of reaction on the part of the State toward crime, one which in other countries has long been part of the penal law: the suspension of the execution of sentence in favor of probation under specified conditions and directions, imposed upon the convict during the time of probation for the purpose of rehabilitation (Sec. 23 et seq.).

In introducing the probation system, the German legislator was guided by old reform wishes resting on the conviction that the short term of imprisonment does more harm than good and should, therefore, be avoided whenever a resocialization (or rehabilitation) of the perpetrator appears propitious. The reform of the fine system in 1924 already had dealt with this consideration, (specifically) by providing in Sec. 27b that, in lieu of a term of imprisonment of less than three months, a fine may be imposed whenever such is sufficient to accomplish the purpose of punishment. In these cases, then, the perpetrator is spared the onus of serving his term of imprisonment.

The introduction of the probation system follows exactly the same path by giving the court the opportunity (in the case of all punishments of less than nine months' detention) to suspend the execution of the sentence and to give the perpetrator the opportunity to exempt himself from the service of the sentence by good conduct on probation.

This solution amounts to a certain synthesis between two corresponding institutions from different cultural spheres, the "sursis" of the French law, and the probation system of the Anglo–American law. The punishment is imposed, the perpetrator is convicted, but the execution is suspended in order to give him the opportunity for rehabilitation. If, during this time, he fulfills the duties imposed upon him and otherwise conducts himself in an impeccable manner, the court, by special decree, will extinguish the punishment. Otherwise it will recall the suspension and order execution of the sentence.

IV.

Because of innumerable definitions, it is hardly possible to give more than a cursory introduction to the Special Part of the penal code. We have already discussed the systematic order in which the various offenses appear. But it is not a very clear structure and remains unsatisfactory. In any event, a study of the norms will reveal the legislators' endeavor to place the determination of the extent of the punishment and other reactions to crime largely within the sphere of judicial activity. While it was clear from the outset that, in the case of the prerequisites of punishment, the principle of legality demands a highly exact and final stand on the law, there never was any doubt that the *conse-quences* of crime could not possibly be as clearly and exactly regulated by the code. Rather, the judge has to enjoy a certain amount of freedom for the exercise of his discretion within the legislative framework of punishments.

It is true that this (vagueness) results in a loss of some certainty and uniformity in the yardsticks with which the penal law is administered. But, on the other hand, an absolutely determined punishment could lead to the greatest injustices. In view of this fact the legislator has provided a kind of compromise. He did not limit himself to the definition of a certain type of crime—for example, larceny, robbery, assault and battery, etc.—leaving the entire evaluation of the punishment to the judge; but rather, he considered the actual typical modes of perpetration of these crimes by recognizing, besides the basic modes of perpetration with their conceptional minimal requirements, all those circumstances which may act in (either) mitigation or aggravation. For these he posited a new and different frame of punishment.

For example, besides the basic form of larceny (Sec. 242), there is grand larceny (Sec. 243), and then a lesser mode of perpetration of larceny in case of need (Sec. 248a), as well as the minor larceny of perishables for personal consumption (Sec. 270 (5)). In the original form of the penal code, the distinctions under which a more serious mode of perpetration could be found were regulated casuistically by the law itself, while, in the case of mitigating circumstances, the code omitted special characterizations leading to the application of the mitigated frame of punishment, and left it entirely to judicial discretion to find such cases. However, practical application soon led to a recognition that the attempt (on the part) of the law to circumscribe the multifariousness of life with certitude led to serious shortcomings because a defect in the law necessarily resulted in gaps and these, ultimately, meant unequal treatment in equal cases. For example, grand larceny is subject to imprisonment in a penitentiary when an automobile is broken into and an object *inside* the automobile is stolen. However, it is only a case of ordinary larceny to break into the automobile in order to steal it, the car itself including all its contents.

Such provisions (in the law) necessarily made for a certain skepticism about the utility of any legislative attempt to determine ultimately the (proper) evaluations in this sphere. The development is clearly in the direction of leaving it to judicial discretion to determine the cases which should be regarded as aggravating. Thus, the legislator seems to have decided to forego the legislative determination of the evaluation of aggravating and/or mitigating circumstances.

In this case we detect, then, an earnest endeavor in the German Penal Code to find a synthesis between legislative certainty as to the penal law and judicial discretion—i.e., to bring into an optimal relation the demands of justice and (the pressures) of legal certainty. Obviously, as a result of this skepticism about the justice of legislative and unalterable axiological decisions, it will remain impossible to create ultimate harmony in this respect. Nevertheless, the tendency to enlarge the sphere of judicial discretion, in a manner going way beyond the ideals of the liberal theory of state, is clearly discernible.

APPENDIX D

BASIC PRINCIPLES OF NORWEGIAN
SUBSTANTIVE CRIMINAL LAW [7]

1. The Rule of Law

THE NORWEGIAN CONSTITUTION of May 17, 1814 has laid down expressly that *no one may be arrested and detained in prison* except in cases stated by the law, and only in the way prescribed by the law. For unwarranted arrest, or unlawful detainment, the person concerned will be responsible to the detained.

The main statutory grounds for arrest are in brief: apprehension *in flagrante delicto;* danger of suspect's escaping, particularly if he is a person of no fixed abode or means of identification; danger of his tampering with the evidence; danger of his repeating the crime or offense; danger of his completing a merely attempted punishable act. Pre–trial detention in jail can be imposed only by judicial order.

It has been laid down by the Constitution that *search and seizure shall not take place except in criminal cases.* In implementation of this provision, the Law on Court Procedure in Criminal Cases regulates the carrying out of searches and seizures. The person and lodging, as well as other premises of an individual, who on good and sufficient grounds is suspected of having committed a punishable act for which more severe punishment than fines may be inflicted, may be searched in order to apprehend the offender, uncover clues to the crime or to accomplish (bring about) a seizure. Premises of other persons may be searched if they were the scene of the crime or of the apprehension of the criminal, or are entered in hot pursuit, or appear to contain the wanted person, an object which may be seized, or clues to the

---

7. Adapted from the Royal Norwegian Ministry of Justice (ed.), *Administration of Justice in Norway* (Oslo: Ministry of Justice, 1957), pp. 119–133.

crime. Searches ordinarily require the consent of the person involved, or a judicial search warrant stating grounds, purpose and object of the search. If there is danger in delaying the action, an order from the public prosecutor may suffice in lieu of a court order. Buildings and premises may be searched *without warrant or order* when in hot pursuit, or when a delay (to secure the needed warrant) would obviously frustrate the intended purposes, provided there is grave suspicion of a crime which may be punished with imprisonment for a period of more than six months. A policeman may, for the purpose of executing a warrant of arrest, search the lodging and premises of the suspect without any special authorization. Searches must be conducted by personnel of the Court, the Public Prosecution, or the Police, in the presence of at least one witness and the owner of the premises or, in his absence, of a member of the household or a neighbor, if readily available, and must upon request be preceded by a reading or display of the warrant, or in lieu thereof, by an explanatory statement.

Written communications between the accused and persons in privileged relation may not be seized in the possession of the latter without their consent, unless they are suspected of complicity. Prospective witnesses may be ordered by the court to surrender evidential material in their possession or to bring it with them and produce it at the trial, and may for that purpose be served *a subpoena duces tecum.* The Court may by judicial decision direct the seizure of mail and telegrams addressed to, or destined for, or originating from, a person who is under reasonable suspicion of having committed a punishable act for which imprisonment for a period of more than six months may be inflicted, provided seizure thereof appears necessary under the circumstances. This does not include correspondence between the accused and his defense counsel.

The maxim *Nullum crimen sine lege, nulla poena sine lege* is an indispensable principle of Norwegian administration of criminal justice. The Constitution has expressly laid down that no one may be convicted except according to law, or be punished except according to judicial sentence. The term "law" as used here implies: (1) formal **laws** (statutes) passed by the Norwegian Parliament ("Stortinget") and assented to by the King in Council; (2) **provisional decrees** with the force of law passed by the King in Council according to the Constitution which provides that the King may make or repeal decrees concerning commerce, customs, trade and industry, and police matters. Such decrees must not be at variance with the Constitution, or with the laws passed by the Parliament, and they shall be provisionally operative only until the termination of the next session of the Parliament, unless previously abrogated by Parliament; (3) **supplementary regulations** of a substantive penal law character issued by subordinate State or municipal organs, when positively empowered to do so by special provision of formal law, such as traffic, rationing and price regulations, etc. With regard to regulations of the latter kind, however, it is either the particular provision of the formal law in question, or the general penal provision laid down by the Penal Code, which forms the basic substantive penal provision, denouncing the unlawful acts or omissions as punishable, and fixing the maximum penalty which may be inflicted (usually fines).

In practice it has been established as a leading rule that the formal law, provisional decree or regulation in question, must have been "duly promulgated" before it comes into force. Accordingly all such provisions will be promulgated in the *Norwegian Law Gazette* ("Norsk lovtidend"). The provisions so promulgated will come into force all over the country four weeks subsequent to the publishing of that issue of the *Gazette* in which the provisions in question have been promulgated, provided the law, or provisional decree, or regulation in question, does not itself stipulate otherwise.

It follows from what has been said above that *bills of attainder* would clearly be at variance with the Constitution. No such bill has ever been passed since the Norwegian Constitution was enacted in 1814.

Although no positive provision to this effect has been expressly laid down by the Constitution, or by formal law, it has always been an unquestioned principle of Norwegian jurisprudence and legislature that any formal law, provisional decree, or any other provision of substantive law, which renders unlawful and punishable an act or omission, must set out in detail the factual and mental prerequisites which constitute the offense or crime in question.

The prohibition against enactment of *ex–post–facto* laws is also an unshakable principle of Norwegian criminal law and justice. It has been laid down by the Constitution that no law may, to the detriment of the accused, be given retroactive effect. As a corollary to this principle, the General Civil Penal Code provides that if the penal laws have been amended during the space of time elapsed since the act was committed, the penal clauses which were in force at the time when the act was committed shall be applied. However, the provisions of penal law in force at the time when a question is pending its decision shall be applied, if such application will lead to a decision more favorable to the accused.

2. Mental and Factual Prerequisites to Criminal Liability, etc.

The maxim *Actus non facit reum nisi mens sit rea* is another principle of Norwegian criminal law and justice.

It has been laid down by the General Civil Penal Code that its penal clauses cannot be brought to bear if the accused did not act willfully, unless it is positively provided, or unambiguously implied, by the penal clause in question, that the inadvertent commission of the act be punishable as well. "Offenses" consisting of omissions are, however, punishable also when committed inadvertently, unless a provision to the contrary has been laid down, or is unambiguously implied by the penal clause in question.

The term "willfully" implies that the accused did in fact have foresight of the natural consequences of his conduct or omission. The term "inadvertently" implies that the person charged ought to have had foresight of the consequences of his conduct or of his omission of such action.

In some cases it is conditional to criminal liability that the act be committed in order to realize or further the fulfillment of a certain stated "intention." In other cases the presence of a certain stated intention is to be considered as an aggravating circumstance. In other cases, again, a certain stated motivating intention may lead to a reduction of the punishment, or even to an exemption from criminal liability.

In consequence of the above mentioned maxim—and as a supplementary safeguard against unjust application of provisions of penal law of whose existence, although duly promulgated, the accused may have had justifiable reasons to be ignorant—it has been laid down by the General Civil Penal Code that if a person, when committing an unlawful act, was ignorant of its illegal character, the punishment may—if the Court does not acquit him for that reason—be reduced below the minimum punishment fixed for that particular crime or offense, or be commuted into a more lenient form of punishment. Beside this provision, pertaining to *ignorance of the law*, the General Civil Penal Code contains another general provision relating to *mistake of facts*. By the latter it has been provided that if a person, when committing an unlawful act, was ignorant of factual circumstances which are conditional to, or aggravating the punishability of, the act, such circumstances shall not be charged to him. If the ignorance may in itself be charged to the accused as inadvertency, the punishment laid down for the inadvertent commission of the act shall be brought to bear. Mistake as to the economic value of an object, or as to the amount to which a damage caused must be assessed, shall be taken into consideration only if the punishability is made conditional thereof. In cases where it has been laid down by the law that increased punishment be brought to bear if a punishable act leads to a certain stated consequence outside his *mens rea*, such increased punishment shall be applied only if the person charged could have foreseen the possibility of such a consequence, or if he has failed to avert it to the best of his ability after he had become aware of the danger.

A person is not subject to criminal liability if he was *insane* or *unconscious* at the time when the act was committed. If his unconsciousness was self-inflicted—whether willfully or inadvertently by way of intoxication (caused by alcohol or by other means)—such unconsciousness does not, however, exempt him from criminal liability.

The punishment may be reduced below the minimum term of punishment fixed by the law for the particular "crime" or "offense" in question if, for instance, the act has been committed under the influence of *justifiable indignation, coercion,* or *imminent danger,* or under the influence of a transient substantial *impairment of consciousness,* provided it was not caused by self–inflicted intoxication.

No one may be punished for an act which he has committed in order to save a person, or property, from a threatening danger otherwise unavoidable, provided the circumstances rendered it justifiable that he considered such danger to be exceptionally imminent in proportion to the damage which might be caused by his act. Besides this *defense of necessity* there is the *plea of justifiable self-defense.* Thus, no one is liable to punishment for any act committed in justifiable self–defense. The General Civil Penal Code defines justifiable self–defense as follows: it shall be considered justifiable self–defense if an act, otherwise punishable, has been committed in order to avert, or to defend oneself against an unlawful attack, provided the act in question does not exceed what seemed necessary to attain this purpose, and provided—when taking into consideration the dangerousness of the attack, the guilt of the assailant, or the character of the legal right attacked—it can no more be deemed decidedly improper to inflict an evil as great as that intended by the act in question. Even if a person has in fact exceeded the limits set by the law for justifiable self–defense, he shall nevertheless be exempted from punishment, provided such overstepping of the limits is solely due to the agitation or consternation provoked by the assault.

3. Attempted "Crimes" and "Offenses"

An attempt at committing a "crime" is punishable. It is deemed to be a punishable attempt if an act has been committed whereby the crime—although not itself accomplished—was *intended* to be accomplished. An attempt to commit an "offense" is, however, not punishable, unless otherwise positively provided. The punishability of attempted crimes ceases to operate if the guilty person of his own free will *either* abstains from the criminal activities in question before the attempt can be considered accomplished, *or* if he averts the consequence, the occurrence of which would render the crime itself accomplished, before he is yet aware that his criminal activities have been discovered.

An attempted crime is subjected to a more lenient punishment than the accomplished crime. The punishment may be reduced below the minimum term of punishment fixed for the accomplished crime, to a more lenient form of punishment. The maximum term of punishment laid down for the accomplished crime may, however, be imposed if the attempt has resulted in a consequence which would have justified the infliction of such a severe punishment, had the consequence in question been within the *mens rea* of the accused.

4. Complicity

An accomplice to a "crime" or an "offense"—no matter whether the *complicity* amounts to what is in English juridico–technical terminology called "a principal in the first or the second degree," or "an accessory before the fact"—will, if made punishable by the penal clause in question, as a rule be liable to the same punishment as that laid down for the principal commission of the punishable act under similar circumstances. If the penal clause does not contain any express provision as to the punishability of complicity, it will depend upon a concrete interpretation of the penal clause in question whether complicity be punishable or not.

It has been provided by the General Penal Code that where more persons have co–operated in achieving a punishable purpose, the punishment may be reduced below the minimum term fixed for the act in question, and be substituted by a more lenient form of punishment, in the case of those whose complicity was to a substantial degree caused by their dependent relation to any of the other guilty persons, or if their complicity has been of inconsiderable importance compared with that of the others. Where the punishment might otherwise have been fixed by imposing a fine, as in the case of "offenses," an accomplice may under such circumstances even be exempted from punishment.

5. Geographical and Personal Range of Norwegian Criminal Law

Regardless of the national status of the offender, Norwegian provisions of substantive criminal law will be applicable to acts committed within the realm, inclusive of Norwegian vessels on the high seas and Norwegian aircraft outside areas subjected to the sovereignty of any particular state. Similarly, they will apply to any punishable act committed on board Norwegian vessels or aircraft, wherever they may be located, by members of their crew or by others who accompany such vessels and aircraft. They will also be brought to bear on punishable acts committed abroad by a Norwegian citizen, or by someone who is resident in Norway, provided the punishable act charged comes within certain categories of crimes or offenses particularly enumerated by the law. The same applies if the act in question constitutes a crime or offense against the Norwegian State or Norwegian State authority, or if the act is punishable also according to the laws of the country where it was committed. Norwegian provisions of substantive criminal law will finally be applicable to punishable acts committed in a foreign country by a foreigner, provided the punishable act charged *either* comes within certain categories of crimes and offenses particularly enumerated by the law, *or* constitutes a crime which is punishable also according to the laws of the country where the act was committed, and provided (in the latter case) that the offender is resident or staying in Norway.

Some Fundamental Safeguards of a Defendant in Norwegian Criminal Procedure

With a view to assisting the foreign student of Norwegian administration of criminal justice in grasping the true nature of this system of criminal law and criminal procedure, it may serve the purpose to give a brief collective survey of the fundamental safeguards of a defendant under Norwegian criminal procedure. In so doing one cannot avoid repeating some of these safeguards (already mentioned in passing reference), in order to complete the picture; particularly insofar as such fundamental safeguards are based upon, or derived from, provisions of a substantive criminal law—, i.e. of a constitutional, statutory, and customary law.

In the following exposition only those fundamental safeguards will be dealt with which are of a procedural character, and which are more or less directly based on the general "Law on Court Procedure in Criminal Cases" and its interpretation in practice. In this context it should be stressed that the provisions of this law are applicable to pre–trial criminal investigation—whether extrajudicial (police) or judicial investigation—as well as to criminal proceedings in the trial Courts.

1. *Right to Be Informed of the Charge*

The person charged or accused should, on his first appearing before the Court, at the latest, *be informed of the nature and cause of the charge* against him. Thus the formal charge or indictment should indicate, as accurately as possible, time, place, object, etc., and describe the act involved. It should furthermore stress the characteristic features prescribed by the law and make reference to the particular provision or provisions of substantive criminal law presumed to be applicable.

When a man suspected of a crime has been arrested on one of the statutory grounds, he has the right to be informed of the judicial warrant of arrest, or of the order of the public prosecutor, issued in lieu thereof, where there is danger in delaying action. The warrant should be displayed or read to him at the time of apprehension or as soon as possible thereafter. The warrant, or order, should precisely designate the suspect, state the crime or offense charged, the ground for the measures taken, and the judge before whom the suspect will be brought. The detained has the right to be brought before the designated judge as soon as possible, or, if this is not feasible, before the nearest examining judge or public prosecutor. If he has not been brought before the judge within twenty–four hours, the reasons therefore must be put on record by the Court. If the Court decides that the arrested person be remanded in custody, it must at the same time fix a certain time limit within which the prosecution must either request the opening of preliminary judicial investigation of the case, or serve the formal indictment on the defendant. Otherwise the arrested person must be set free, unless the time limit is prolonged by the Court.

During pre–trial judicial examination, which is a prerequisite in jury trials, the prosecution must communicate to the accused, or his counsel (if any), all available information and exhibits pertaining to the case without delay. The accused and his counsel have the right to inspect the judicial records and police documents relating to the case at any stage of the proceedings. They should be informed of the conclusion or discontinuance of the pre–trial examination.

In cases which come within the jurisdiction of the Court of Appeals, the accused, or a mere suspect, may petition the Court to take judicial steps in order to have the suspicion against him dispelled.

2. Right to Be Present at the Trial; Right to Have a Counsel of Defense; etc.

The accused has the right to be present at the trial. Actually the accused is under obligation to be present as long as he has the right to express himself. He may, however, be allowed to withdraw when he has given evidence in his own behalf and until pronouncement of sentence.

The Court may decide that an accused shall leave the court-room during the questioning of a witness or of a co–accused, if there are particular reasons to fear that an unreserved statement cannot otherwise be obtained. If an accused has withdrawn from the courtroom for such reasons, he may demand that the questioning be repeated after he has been recalled. He shall at any rate be made acquainted with what has occurred during his absence.

The person charged, or the accused, has the right to have the assistance of a counsel for his defense at any stage of the criminal investigation and during the subsequent criminal proceedings. In jury cases he may even brief more than one counsel for the trial. If the person charged is under fifteen years of age, the choice of counsel rests with his guardian. The assistance of such counsel is obligatory, unless otherwise specifically provided, with regard to any kind of case:

a. at the main hearing of the case before the trial Court, as well as during preliminary judicial examination of witnesses, and during preliminary judicial examination and recording of other evidence, provided such evidence may be, or is intended to be used during the trial;

b. during Court sittings from which the accused has been excluded for some particular reason laid down by the law.

In the cases mentioned above a State–appointed counsel shall be briefed by the Court on its own initiative at the expense of the public. As a rule the counsel already briefed or chosen by the accused will be briefed also and thus obtain the status of a State–appointed counsel.

In cases other than those mentioned above, a counsel for the defense will be briefed by the Court on its own initiative only when it is deemed necessary on account of the extraordinary character of the case at hand, and provided so requested by the accused.

Persons who are charged together and whose interests are mutually conflicting cannot be represented by the same joint counsel at their joint trial.

If the accused does not know, or is not conversant with the Norwegian language, or if he is deaf, he is *entitled to have the assistance of a competent interpreter.* The interpreter will in such a case be appointed or authorized by the Court on its own initiative. If necessitated by the importance of the case, the Court may decide that the recording shall take place in the foreign language as well, in order to be entered in the official Court records, or as a special appendix, and be presented for approval.

The services of an interpreter are not necessary if the members of the Court and the Court witness appointed by authority, as well as the parties to the case, have command of the foreign language in question.

During police investigations and preliminary judicial investigations in criminal cases, the services of an interpreter are not necessary if the judge himself knows the foreign language in question.

If the accused is an alien, there is nothing to prevent a *representative of the foreign government concerned* from attending the court sittings and the trial. Apart from the accused's right to have the assistance of a counsel for his defense at any stage of the proceedings, one or more individually stated representatives of the foreign country concerned may, and would certainly, as a rule, obtain special permission from the court to be present, and to safeguard the interests of the accused jointly with the duly briefed counsel. The provisions in force pertaining to the legal status of a counsel proper would, however, not be applicable to such assisting representatives, whether alien or Norwegian subjects.

From the above it follows that the accused would also, as a rule, be free to communicate with any such representative.

3. *Impartiality of the Court.*

The accused is entitled to be tried by an impartial Court.

Elaborate provisions have been laid down by the law to secure the impartiality of judges (inclusive of lay judges), jurors, Court registrars, and expert witnesses appointed by the Court on its own initiative to make investigation and to give evidence. Furthermore there is the general provision that no one may serve as a judge if circumstances are prevailing, other than those particularly enumerated by law, which are likely to impair confidence as to his impartiality. This will, in particular, apply if one of the parties for that reason requests that the judge withdraw from the case.

4. *Bail Pending Trial*

Under Norwegian law pre–trial confinement may be lifted on certain conditions, provided the circumstances offer no particular reasons to fear that evidence will be obstructed by concealment or collusion. The detainment may be lifted by deposition of security (bail), or if the accused promises not to leave a stated place of residence, or pledges to report to the Police at stated times, etc. If the act charged cannot lead to a more severe punishment than imprisonment for a period of up to six months, the accused is entitled to be released or exempted from pre–trial confinement, subject to security.

The course and headway of the criminal proceedings is subject to constant check and control by the prosecution, by the judge of the trial Court, as well as by the accused himself and his counsel of defense. The time limits set by the law for the application of legal remedies are short, and must be strictly adhered to by the parties concerned.

APPENDIX E

RULES GOVERNING RELATIONS BETWEEN LOCAL POLICE AUTHORITIES AND POLICE COMMITTEES IN SWEDEN [8]

Introductory Provision

Section 1

There shall be a Police Committee in every Police District for consultation with the Chief of Police on matters of general importance to the Police of the District.

Functions of the Police Committee

Section 2

To the Chief of Police, Committee shall submit the proposals and otherwise state the views that it deems required in order to encourage relations of trust between the Police and the general public. When requested by the Chief of Police the Police Committee shall submit its comments on matters concerning the police establishment of the district.

Structure of the Police Committee, etc.

Section 3

The Police Committee shall consist of nine members and an equal number of substitute members. When the Police District covers no more than Five municipal areas, Committee members and their deputies shall be elected by the Councils of the municipal areas, and otherwise by representatives of the municipal areas included in the Police District.

Section 4

Representatives and substitute representatives shall be elected by the Municipal Councils. The election shall take place no later than November 15 of the year following the year in which general elections for the Councils took place. The order in which substitutes shall be called upon for service shall be determined at the election.

Section 5

Each municipal area shall appoint one representative for each whole or partial population figure of 30,000 or whatever lower figure that is required to bring the number of reresentatives for the whole Police

---

8. National Swedish Police Board, Information Division, 1968.

District up to 18 as a minimum. No municipal area may, however, appoint more than 10 representatives. Each municipal area shall appoint as many substitutes as it appoints representatives.

The County Administrative Board shall determine the number of representatives of each municipal area in good time before the election takes place.

Section 6

The provisions relating to Municipal Councils laid down in the Municipal Law shall apply with regard to eligibility as representative or substitute representative, the loss of eligibility, and the right of non-acceptance.

Section 7

Representatives and substitute representatives shall be elected for a period of Four years, calculated from November 16 of the year in which the election took place. If a representative resigns or departs from life before the expiration of this period, the substitute representative who should take precedence according to the order determined at the election, shall be called upon. If there is no substitute representative to replace him/her, a new election of representative and substitute representative for the remaining period of the mandate shall be held.

The County Administrative Board shall be informed immediately of elections of representatives and substitute representatives, the names and addresses of those elected being stated.

Section 8

Persons domiciled within the Police District and entitled to vote in municipal elections are eligible as members or substitute members of Police Committees. The provisions relating to Municipal Councils laid down in the Municipal Law shall apply with regard to other qualifications for eligibility, the loss of eligibility, and the right of non-acceptance.

Section 9

Members and substitute members of Police Committees are elected for Four years, calculated from the first of January of the year following the year during which the election took place. The election shall be held in December of the year following the year in which elections of municipal Councils took place.

Where members and substitute members of the Police Committees are to be elected by Municipal Councils in several municipal areas, each area shall elect one member and one substitute member for each whole or partial population figure required to secure the number of members and substitute members laid down in Section 3. The County Administrative Board shall determine the number of members and substitute members to be appointed by each municipal area in good time before the election is due to take place.

The Police Committee determines the order in which substitute members shall be called upon to do service. If a member resigns or departs from life before the expiration of his/her mandate and there is no substitute member to replace him/her, a new election of member and substitute member for the remaining period of the mandate shall be held. In cases envisaged in the second subsection, the election is held by the Municipal Council that appointed the original member.

Section 10

Where the election of members and substitute members of a Police Committee is to be carried out by representatives, the County Administrative Board appoints a time and a place for the election and summons the representatives to the election. The County Administrative Board appoints one of the representatives to conduct proceedings until a chairman has been elected. The election may be held if at least half the number of appointed representatives are present. The election proceedings are led by a chairman elected by the representatives.

Section 11

The provisions laid down the reimbursement of members of Municipal Councils, and committees shall apply to the reimbursement of representatives and substitute representatives.

Section 12

At the election of members of a Police Committee, one member shall be appointed convener and lead the proceedings until a chairman has been elected. Where members are elected by the Councils of several municipal areas, the convener is appointed by the County Administrative Board.

Section 13

Should the boundaries of the Police District become modified the County Administrative Board has to direct the election of a new Police Committee.

Section 14

Notice of the election of a Police Committee and the convener, where a convener was appointed at the election, as well as of the chairman, the vice-chairman, and the secretary of the Committee shall be given promptly to the County Administrative Board for publication in the County Gazette.

Meetings of Police Committees

Section 15

The provisions of the Municipal Law relating to Municipal Councils and committees and in the case of the Stockholm Police District the provisions of the Local Government Act for Stockholm shall apply to meetings of Police Committees and their activities in general, with those exceptions that are mentioned in the said laws.

The Chief of Police shall be informed of the time and place of meetings of the Police Committee.

Section 16

The County Police Commissioner and the local Chief of Police are entitled to attend meetings and to take part in discussions but not in decisions.

The Chief of Police, or, in the event of the Chief of Police being prevented from attending, the senior police officer whom he appoints in his place, shall attend meetings of the Police Committee and provide information requested by the Committee or its chairman.

Section 17

For attendance at meetings of Police Committees members are entitled to a remuneration, the reimbursement of travel costs, as well as a daily allowance from State Funds on the same principles as those laid down for jurors attending sessions of district courts. In addition, the chairman is entitled to reimbursement from State Funds of necessary expenses in connection with the work of the Committee.

Compensation is paid out by the County Administrative Board.

Appeals

Section 18

Appeals against decisions of Police Committees and against elections carried out by representatives are lodged with the County Administrative Board. The provisions relating to appeals against decisions of Municipal Councils and other municipal committees shall apply.

With the exceptions listed below, this Act shall come into force on January 1, 1965.

Elections of representatives and substitute representatives shall take place the first time in 1964 and shall refer to the period November 16, 1964–November 15, 1967.

Elections of members and substitute members of Police Committees shall take place the first time in 1964 and shall refer to the period January 1, 1965–December 31, 1967.

By this all whom it may concern obediently shall abide. In faith whereof We have set Our hand hereunto and in confirmation thereof affixed Our Royal Seal.

APPENDIX F

OFFENSES SUBJECT TO THE JURISDICTION OF THE
SWISS NATIONAL GOVERNMENT
(Article 340 of the Penal Code)

The illegal use of explosives or poison gas.

Offenses involving counterfeit money, forgery of official stamps, seals, marks, or falsification of weights and measures.

Forgery of official bonds.

Offenses against the national security.

Offenses against the will of the people at federal elections and in connection with federal voting.

Offenses against the administration of federal justice.

Offenses against the authorities or officials of the national government.

Offenses compromising relations with other countries.

Offenses committed by the authorities or officials in connection with their duties.

The violation of military secrets, trafficking in material sequestrated or requisitioned by the army or unauthorized wearing of military uniform.

Political offenses resulting in or following disturbances involving intervention by the federal army.

These offenses are listed in Chapter 1 of Article 340 of the penal code. Chapter 2 of the same article lays down that offenses against provisions of certain special federal laws shall come under federal jurisdiction. They are chiefly:

The law of December 21, 1958, on air navigation.

The law of December 23, 1953, on the national bank.

The law of October 14, 1922, on telegraphic and telephonic communication.

The law of October 5, 1929, on the postal service.

The law of December 17, 1952, on currency.

The order of the Federal Council on March 28, 1949, concerning war materials.

INDEX

223